Writers in Sussex

G000138528

WRITERS IN
SUSSEX

Bernard Smith & Peter Haas
Foreword by Christopher Fry

REDCLIFFE
Bristol

First published in 1985
by Redcliffe Press Ltd.,
49 Park St., Bristol

Text © Bernard Smith
Photographs © Peter Haas

ISBN 0905 459 97 0

All rights reserved. No part of this publication
may be reproduced, stored in a retrieval
system, or transmitted, in any form or by any
means, electronic, mechanical, photocopying,
recording or otherwise, without the prior
permission of the publishers.

Typeset by Folio Photosetting, Bristol
Printed and bound by Eyre and Spottiswoode Ltd.

Contents

Foreword

About thirty years ago I found in a second-hand bookshop a London Street Directory for 1871 (the year my mother was born) and at leisure moments in the months that followed I made a list of the addresses of people I should have been interested to meet if my life had begun a hundred years sooner than it did. It gave some kind of extension to time, to stand at the door of 62 Avenue Road and know that Gounod had come to the house after the first night of *Faust*, or to know that my second-cousin and the actor Macready both lived in Clarence Terrace, Regent's Park.

Since we can't yet take the Wellsian Time Machine into the future we can at least glance over the backward limit of our consciousness and get glimpses of what has gone before. And for that we need a guide, and what better guide in Sussex than Bernard Smith? In 1936 my wife and I went to live in an old mill-house at Coleman's Hatch. We knew that not far away were the A.A. Milnes at Cotchford Farm. What we didn't know, until Bernard Smith told us, was that twenty-three years earlier W.B. Yeats and Ezra Pound had rented a cottage even nearer to where we were living. Every time we had driven to Forest Row we had passed the end of the lane which would have led us to Stone Cottage.

The pages of this book give us the sign-posts we need, and the essence of the lives of those men and women whose homes we may seek out. Some I know well already. Each time we have gone into the chemist's shop in Midhurst we have dipped into the boyhood and apprenticeship of H.G. Wells. All the place-names that Belloc mentions 'in place of a prayer', we share with him now, and often take a look at Courthill Farm on our way to buy a pumpkin at Slindon, passing on our way William Hayley's house at Eartham. And the chapter of the book which gives me the sensation of belonging (as I do indeed almost belong) to time-past rather than time-present, is the essay on Andrew Young. At Christmas time in 1957 I stayed with Andrew and Janet at Stonegate Vicarage, read one of the lessons at the Carol Service, watched the village children acting a Nativity play (Andrew loved and was loved by children), and after supper listened while Andrew and the poet Christopher Hassall went through together line by line the recently written *A Traveller in Time*.

Then there are the book's surprises. Often enough, after visiting the snowdrops at Iping, we have admired Woolbeding House, but in our thoughts it was tenantless until Bernard Smith people it with Charlotte Smith and her family. And until now Mark Rutherford to me was a townsman of Bedford, as I was, and a pupil at the Modern School, as I was, though seventy-five years divide our schooldays. It was good to come across him again in Sussex. The wide county from east to west has been given a fresh reason for us to explore, to visit those places so splendidly caught by the camera of Peter Haas, and in our minds to reinstate these Sussex dwellers into their old haunts.

Christopher Fry
East Dean 1985

1. John Selden *(1584–1654)* Worthing

Selden was born in Salvington, at the back of Worthing, a separate village at the time but now drowned in the northwards-spreading tide of houses. Worthing guide books used proudly to direct visitors to Selden's birthplace, a thatched, timbered cottage in Selden's Way. The last to mention it appeared in 1955 when it was said to be 'hemmed in by none too picturesque modernity' and in the same year the cottage was badly damaged by fire. It was demolished shortly afterwards. A bungalow, number 17, now stands on the site.

The following description of the cottage is taken from an auctioneer's catalogue of 1923, when Salvington Farm, where the cottage stood, was sold off as building plots.

> Lot 9: The interesting old-fashioned cottage, well known as the reputed dwelling of John Selden. The cottage bears the date 1601 over the entrance door, and there is a Latin inscription carved on the inside of the lintel. The cottage is built of brick and flint with thatched roof, and contains Entrance Passage, Living Room with range, Scullery with copper, Pantry with shelves, and 2 Bedrooms. In the cottage there are some fine Oak

John Selden
17 Selden's Way, Worthing

Doors. Outside there is a brick and flint Fuel House, Privy, Well with Pump and a Garden.

Selden's parents were very ordinary people; in the register of West Tarring Church where John was baptized, his father is described as a 'minstrell'. They soon recognised that young John was exceptionally talented: the Latin inscription in the lintel, mentioned in the auctioneer's description, was written by John when he was ten years old and was translated by Dr. Johnson:

> Walk in and welcome, honest friend, repose,
> Thief, get thee hence: to thee I'll not unclose.

They sent him to the Prebendal School in Chichester which is still there in West Street and from there he went to Oxford and London to study law.

Although he was called to the bar he was never much interested in the practice of law; it was the study of the history of law and the early history of England that became his passion. He made friends with Ben Jonson the dramatist and with Sir Robert Cotton, the antiquary. Cotton lived in a house where the House of Lords now stands and filled it with one of the biggest private collections of books, manuscripts and coins in England. Cotton was ahead of his time in realising the importance to historians of charters and rolls. In a tailor's shop he picked up a discarded bit of parchment which turned out to be an original copy of Magna Carta. When he died, his manuscripts became the nucleus of the British Museum collection. He gave Selden the freedom of his library and fired him with his own enthusiasm for research. Selden had a prodigious memory and worked incessantly; at the age of twenty-six he published three books, all in Latin and all immensely erudite, on the early history of England. These were followed by the massive *Titles of Honour*, the forerunner of today's *Debrett's Peerage* and, in 1617, *History of Tithes*, the book that changed him overnight from an almost unknown scholar into the most talked-about man in London.

It was a time when the power of King and Church were being questioned and both were exceedingly touchy. Selden's book upset them by denying the divine right of the clergy to exact tithes. He claimed that he was not hostile to the Church but merely writing history. This did nothing to soothe the bishops who wanted the book suppressed. Selden was hauled before the Court of High Commission which demanded an apology; cleverly, Selden apologised for the book's publication but not for its contents. The book was suppressed and he was forbidden to answer any attack made either upon the book or upon himself. This unjust treatment aroused in Selden a strong resistance to dictatorial government and from then on he used the motto 'Liberty before all things' in his books.

A few years later, Selden entered politics as a Member of Parliament and was soon taking a leading part in the great debates on the liberty of the subject and the freedom of Parliament from royal interference. Selden was in great demand by the disputants because his knowledge of English law and history was rivalled only by the great Sir

Edward Coke. He appeared as counsel for Sir Edmund Hampden who had refused to lend money to King Charles the First and in 1628 he helped Coke and Sir John Eliot to draw up the famous Petition of Right. As a result, he and Eliot were sent to the Tower of London for two years.

King Charles had now dissolved parliament and was ruling without it; opposition to the King was dangerous so Selden prudently withdrew from politics – 'The wisest way for men in these times is to say nothing' he privately remarked. He now began exploring Hebrew and oriental culture, collecting works in Turkish, Persian and the Chinese languages. He wrote fluently in Arabic as well as in Latin and Greek. He also became a specialist in Hebrew law and published several weighty volumes on the subject. John Milton, his contemporary, referred to him as, 'The Chief of Learned men reputed in this land'.

Did Selden ever marry? Gossips of the time made much of the fact that he was the Earl of Kent's steward and very friendly with the Countess Dowager. When the Earl died, Selden continued to manage the estate at Wrest, in Bedfordshire, and to spend long holidays there. He also lived in her London mansion and was gratified when he heard that she had willed her personal estate to him. When he died he left £40,000, a fortune in those days.

'If learning could have kept a man alive, this our brother had not died.' The remark was made by someone at his graveside; it would have made a fitting epitaph. His library of 8,000 books was moved to the Bodleian Library at Oxford. When the books were unpacked, several pairs of spectacles were found between the pages; Selden used them as bookmarks and forgot where he put them. Twenty-five years after his death his only book written in English was published: *Table-Talk* preserves Selden's comments on a variety of subjects, made in the company of his friends and noted down by his secretary.

The site of Selden's cottage is north of the Littlehampton Road (A2302), near Becket's Corner. The only bit of the cottage to survive is the lintel that bears the Latin inscription. It languishes in a dusty storeroom in Worthing's museum. Brewers have done more for Selden than anyone else: there are two local pubs that commemorate him. The John Selden pub is in the Salvington Road, a few minutes walk from where Selden was born, its signboard having a very attractive portrait of him. In West Tarring Church there is a small tablet to Selden although he is buried in the Temple Church in London where a memorial describes him as 'the great dictator of learning to the English nation'.

In his famous Dictionary Dr. Johnson brackets the exciseman with the political pamphleteer as 'the two lowest of human beings'. What would he have thought of Tom Paine who was both of these? But Johnson was already dead when the *Rights of Man* was published in 1790.

Lewes nowadays is proud of its association with the man who was once burnt in effigy in scores of villages throughout England. It was at Bull House that Paine lodged when he first arrived in Lewes in 1768 as the town's new excise officer, it then being a tobacco and grocery shop kept by Samuel Ollive. The following year Samuel died leaving his wife and a pretty blonde daughter in poverty. Paine, who had learned from Samuel how to use the tobacco and snuff mills in the cellar of the house, took a share in the business, combining it with his work as exciseman. A couple of years later, he and Elizabeth, the daughter, were married in St. Michael's Church in the High Street – the church with the unusual round tower. He was 34 and she was about ten years younger.

By this time Paine had a reputation in Lewes as a man of vigorously expressed opinions. He was a member of the White Hart Club where educated townsmen met for conversation and debate. Paine had a taste for brandy as well as for argument and he soon established himself as the most witty and entertaining of the Club's debaters. He liked advancing novel views like justice for women, the abolition of slavery, the folly of duelling and the need for international arbitration instead of war. One of his many admirers at this time was young Thomas Rickman, who was later to write a biography of him. It was at the White Hart Club that Paine hammered out the republican views that were later to make him famous.

Dr. Johnson's opinion of excisemen was one that was very generally held in the eighteenth century. Most people from gentry and parson downwards thought that taxes on imported goods like tea, tobacco and spirits should be avoided if at all possible and they had no moral scruples about smuggling. It follows that an exciseman who did his job conscientiously would not be popular; he was more likely to end up in the Ouse marshes with a cracked head. Since Paine thought the exorbitant taxes caused 'numerous and various distresses' he presumably felt justified in neglecting to catch offenders. This seems a more likely explanation of his popularity in Lewes than the theory that he was accepting bribes. It is true that excisemen were so low-paid that bribes were always a temptation but Paine was the least mercenary of men; the profits from his writings were all given away to deserving causes. Besides, if he had been taking bribes he might have paid off his creditors who were now pressing him so hard that he had to shut down his little shop and put his stock, his tobacco and snuff mills and his furniture up to auction.

Tom Paine

Bull House, Lewes

No matter how disordered their own affairs may be, reformers like Tom Paine never lose their enthusiasm for re-ordering the life of society. He now began a national campaign to raise excisemen's wages and wrote his first published work, a pamphlet, *Case of the Officers of Excise*. Like all his writings, it was simple, direct and extremely forceful – it was meant to be read by the common man. His argument was that better pay would discourage bribery and result in a more efficient public service. He invited all excise officers to sign a petition which was later submitted to Parliament. Each exciseman subscribed three shillings, a total of £500. But all his efforts were wasted since Parliament ignored him. His employers, however, did not. They had noticed how much time he was spending going round the country getting up his petition and made this the excuse for ridding themselves of an awkward employee. He was sacked for 'having quitted his Business without obtaining the Board's leave'.

Two months later, he and Elizabeth parted, their marriage having lasted only three years. It had little chance of succeeding since, on top of Tom losing his business and his job, the marriage had been unconsummated. When his friend Rickman asked Paine why his marriage failed, he said: 'It is nobody's business but my own: I had cause for it, but I will name it to no one.' Nor did he. The door had shut and no biographer has yet found a key to open it.

Adversity always brought out the best in Paine: he packed his bags and left for London and later that year, 1774, he sailed for America. There he was to inspire the thirteen states to fight for their independence against King George's red-coats. It was the last Lewes saw of him but not the last it heard of him. In 1790 he was back in London to publish the *Rights of Man*, meeting again his old friend Thomas Rickman who now had a bookshop in the city. The government outlawed Paine as a 'wicked, malicious, seditious, and ill-disposed person' who was trying to overthrow Crown and Parliament and set up a republic. Paine sensibly slipped away to France on a Dover sloop, followed shortly afterwards by Rickman. In many Sussex villages, as elsewhere in England, Paine was burnt in effigy by mobs bribed by the parson or local squire. In Cuckfield in 1793 the villagers sang 'God Save the King' as they burned Paine's effigy and in Shipley in the same year the parish clerk was burned in effigy before his own cottage door for having defended the *Rights of Man*. It was nearly a hundred years before Tennyson would write of England:

It is the land that freemen till
That sober suited freedom chose
The land where, girt with friends or foes,
A man may speak the thing he will.

The three buildings associated with Paine, Bull House, St. Michael's Church and the White Hart are all in the High Street, Lewes.

3. William Hayley   *(1745–1820)*

Eartham &
Felpham

Nowadays it would be difficult to find anyone, anywhere, who has read Hayley's poetry: yet in his own day *The Triumphs of Temper* was a best-seller and ran into fourteen editions. It was elegant verse in the fashion of the time, full of literary artifice, comfortable moralising and sentimental wisdom. Hayley was able to unreel yards of it with appalling ease and soon acquired a reputation far beyond his deserts. At least Robert Southey observed that 'everything about the man was good – except his poetry'.

He lives on as the friend of some of the great men of his age – of William Cowper the poet, of George Romney the painter, of Gibbon the historian. But most of all as the friend of the visionary artist and poet William Blake.

Hayley was Sussex born and bred. His mother was the daughter of the Member of Parliament for Chichester and William was born in the city. His first wife, Eliza, was the daughter of the Dean of Chichester and she and William were married in the cathedral by the Bishop.

At first they lived in London, in Lincoln's Inn Fields, while William tried to get his plays accepted by theatre managers. He had no success so they left London for a small estate at Eartham, near Chichester, which they inherited from William's father. They enlarged the house, laid out a garden and had the surroundings landscaped to provide the poet with rural vistas and distant prospects of the sea. Here William began writing epic poems on almost every imaginable theme, grave and trivial, and contrived to get most of them published. He earned a small but growing income from his verse but they were in no danger of starving as both he and Eliza had private incomes.

The first of his really successful poems was 'The Epistle on Painting' dedicated to Romney. The two men were already friends and Romney had painted Hayley's portrait. The poem helped to make both of them famous and for the next twenty years Romney would spend several weeks in the autumn at Eartham House. He had a little studio built in the grounds and would join Hayley for a dip in the sea, a practice which convinced the villagers that the poet and his friends were mad.

Hayley exerted himself to attract interesting literary people to Eartham. Edward Gibbon, historian of the Roman Empire, who was living at Brighton at the time, was one of them. Hayley referred to him as 'the Roman eagle'. Then there was Flaxman, the sculptor, who, like Gibbon, became a lifelong friend, and others like Charlotte Smith the Sussex poet.

But while Hayley read his elegant verses to his friends and cultivated his literary circle, his marriage was fast breaking up. William referred to his wife as 'pitiable Eliza' and believed she was afflicted with the same mild insanity as her mother. She failed to bear any children and it seems that in desperation they made the same sort of arrangement that Abraham and Sarah of old had made. It was just as successful with

William getting himself a son by Miss Betts, the housemaid. For some years he passed off Thomas Alphonso as his adopted son but he soon dropped the pretence. The boy died after a harrowing illness at the age of 18.

In his memoirs Hayley refers to 'the calamitous pressure of connubial infelicity' – his way of saying that Eliza and he could no longer bear the sight of each other. Sending her to Bath to take the waters was no longer the answer. There had to be a final separation. This was achieved in 1789 after twenty years of married life: they never saw each other again.

It was about this time that Hayley's friendship with the poet Cowper began. Cowper was a melancholic and spent most of his life near the edge of madness. Nights were specially bad times for him: 'I am hunted by spiritual hounds in the night season', he told Hayley. At last Cowper was persuaded to make the journey to Eartham where he stayed for six weeks. 'The most elegant mansion that I have ever inhabited and surrounded by the most delightful pleasure grounds that I have ever seen.' He noted that the Isle of Wight 'may also be seen plainly from the window of the library in which I am writing'. But while Romney, Hayley and young Tom were splashing in the sea, Cowper remained brooding in the library. When he left they were all in tears.

Hayley was genuinely fond of Cowper and tried hard to get him a government pension. The poet, fearful of a recurrence of an earlier fit of madness when he had attempted suicide, was taking ever larger doses of laudanum. When the pension finally came, it was too late – Cowper was dead. Hayley's memorial to his lost friend was his *Life of Cowper*, probably his best work.

After Eliza had gone, Hayley sold Eartham House and moved to Felpham, a village near Bognor. He bought a cottage and enlarged it, making the whole of the first floor into a splendid library filled with books, paintings, busts, and his collection of Chinese porcelain. The house was surrounded by a high cobble wall with a keeper in charge of great iron gates. Venetian blinds were drawn whenever the sun shone to protect Hayley's weak eyesight. It is not surprising that the 'hermit', as he was known, was regarded with some suspicion by the villagers.

In 1800 Hayley persuaded William Blake to move from London to a cottage in Felpham. The story of their friendship and of Blake's trial for sedition at Chichester can be found in the chapter on Blake.

Blake returned to London after three years, leaving an ageing and lonely Hayley. He no longer bathed in the sea on winter mornings and it is doubtful if he still used the new-fangled shower that used to deluge him with icy water every morning. He was still writing with the same thoughtless ease but when his biography of George Romney was published it was a disastrous flop. Most of his old friends were either dead or too old to visit him.

And then, quite suddenly, he met and married Mary Welford. He was 64 and she was 28. Hayley himself admitted that it was a marriage of 'hasty affection rather than deliberate prudence'. For three years they lived together at Turret House and then it

16

William Hayley   *The Orangery, Eartham House, Eartham*

was all over, Mary had gone. No one knows why. There was a persistent rumour in Felpham, surviving almost up to the present day, that her brothers came and took her away because of Hayley's cruelty. He is said to have chained her to an elm tree in the garden.

Hayley hung on to life for another eight years. He wrote his memoirs and arranged with his publisher to pay him an annuity for as long as he lived in return for the right to publish the book after his death. He died at last of a large stone in the bladder and was buried in Felpham Church. On the north wall of the chancel is a slab describing him simply as

The Friend and Biographer of Cowper

There follows an impossibly long epitaph in verse. Hayley, himself a great writer of epitaphs, would have admired it.

Readers using Nairn & Pevsner's Sussex *(1977 ed) should note that it is wrong in saying that Hayley's Turret House at Felpham is still standing: unhappily it was demolished in 1961.*

Hayley's house at Eartham is now Great Ballard School. It was largely rebuilt by Lutyens in 1907 and has little resemblance to the house Hayley knew. But Hayley's library, now a boys' dormitory, is still a splendid room with its Flaxman fireplace and the poet's favourite view of the sea across unspoilt countryside. Standing apart from the house is the Orangery, a bit of Hayley's Eartham which Lutyens left untouched: a charming brick and flint building. Eartham House can be visited by appointment. Telephone the School Secretary on Slindon 360.

17

There is no better lesson in the brevity of literary reputations than the career of Charlotte Smith. In her lifetime she was praised by Sir Walter Scott and Wordsworth and her published novels and poems – all 36 volumes of them – sold well enough to support a large family. Thirty years after her death, Horsfield, in his *History of Sussex*, affirmed that her poems were 'the elegant effusions of true genius'. When another thirty years had passed, Lower, in his *Worthies of Sussex*, had to admit that her novels 'are now little read or even heard of'. He tried to keep a flag flying for her poems which 'live and will live'.

She was born in 1749 at her father's London house in King Street, St. James's Square but spent her childhood at Bignor Park north-east of Chichester. Her mother died when she was three and she was put in the care of an aunt. At six she was packed off to a school at Chichester and later to a more fashionable one in Kensington. When she was 15 years old the obliging aunt arranged for her to be married to Benjamin Smith, whose father had a business in the West Indies.

An early biographer of Charlotte says that her husband 'had never been assiduous in mercantile efforts'; a polite way of saying that he was bone-lazy. For the first ten years of their married life they lived with his parents and while Charlotte waited on the invalid mother, Benjamin sponged on his father. Charlotte now began having a baby every year and by the time she was twenty-five she had had nine children, seven of them surviving. Benjamin thought of trying his luck at farming and they moved to Lys Farm in Hampshire. Two years later, Benjamin's father died and left a will that was meant to benefit his grandchildren. It was so complicated that Charlotte spent the rest of her life haggling with lawyers and executors without getting a penny for her trouble. Legal expenses were added to the debts incurred by Benjamin's disastrous attempts at farming and they soon found themselves committed to the debtors' prison for seven months.

Once released, the family had to keep on the move to escape the numerous creditors. With seven children to feed and clothe, Charlotte must often have known hunger and poverty. What is extraordinary is that she managed to free herself sufficiently from domestic anxieties to write a great deal of poetry. When it was repeatedly rejected by publishers she turned in desperation to the soft-hearted William Hayley (see previous chapter), whose mansion at Eartham was but an hour's walk from her childhood home at Bignor. Hayley allowed her to dedicate her 'Elegiac Sonnets' to him and arranged for them to be printed in Chichester. They were an immediate success and went into five editions in five years.

Quick to scent money, their creditors were now hard on their heels so the family prudently withdrew to a dilapidated chateau in Dieppe. Charlotte busied herself translating Prevost's novel *Manon Lescaut*. When it was safe to return they settled at

Woolbeding House near Midhurst. Charlotte had now made up her mind to separate from her husband and support her family by her pen. It was a brave decision in days when there was no State allowance for children or for single-parent families. She bore Benjamin no grievance; they parted the best of friends, and met occasionally and she even sent him some money. But she firmly refused to live with him.

She got down to the serious business of writing and a year or so later her first novel was published – *Emmeline, or the Orphan of the Castle*. It was another instant success. Encouraged by this, Charlotte began producing novels as regularly as she had once produced children. Over the next ten years she wrote one a year and they sold well enough for her to demand and get advance payments out of her publisher. About this time one of her daughters, who had made an unfortunate marriage, returned home penniless with three hungry children.

For some time Charlotte lived at Brighton. She was there in 1791 when William Wordsworth, waiting for a boat, called on her and admired her sonnets. She became a bit of a blue-stocking, mixing with radical thinkers who read Rousseau and Tom

Charlotte Smith   *Woolbeding House, Woolbeding*

19

Paine. Under their influence she wrote the novel *Desmond* in which she championed the French Revolution and attacked the English monarchy, an unpopular and risky thing to do at that time.

Another of her novels, *The Old Manor House*, republished as recently as 1969, was mostly written at Hayley's house where she stayed for some weeks. She would spend the morning writing in her room and in the evening she would read what she had written to the other guests. George Romney, the portrait painter, was also staying at the house and was greatly impressed by her: 'She wrote a chapter every day, which was read at night, without requiring any correcting. I think her a woman of astonishing powers.' In the afternoons, if the weather was fine, Hayley and his friends would play quoits.

Charlotte went on writing up to the end, dictating to one of her daughters when rheumatism in her hands made holding a pen too painful. She was working on a long poem entitled 'Beachy Head' when she died. She was buried in Stoke Church, Guildford, in Surrey, where many of her father's family lie.

In 1807, the year after her death, the official guide to Bognor included a sonnet of hers about Middleton Church's graveyard which was being rapidly washed away by the encroaching sea: both church and graveyard have now vanished altogether. 'Middleton Church' said the Guide, 'has obtained some celebrity from having furnished the scene of one of the poetical compositions of the late ingenious and unfortunate Mrs Charlotte Smith.' Here are the last few lines:

> With shells and seaweed mingled on the shore,
> Lo' their bones whiten in the frequent wave;
> But vain to them the winds and waters rave;
> They hear the warring elements no more;
> While I am doomed, by life's long storm oppressed,
> To gaze with envy on their gloomy rest!

Woolbeding is a mile or two north-east of Midhurst. Turn north off the A272 at the signpost to Woolbeding. After crossing the hump-backed medieval bridge over the River Rother, pause to enjoy the sight of the south front of Woolbeding House through a gap in the trees. Continue on this winding road and a fine view of the House, which is private, emerges on the right-hand side.

5. William Blake   *(1757–1827)*   Felpham

At six o'clock on a fine September morning in 1800 a chaise stopped outside 13 Hercules Buildings, Lambeth. William Blake, Kate his wife, and his sister Catherine were waiting together with sixteen heavy boxes of paper and copper plates, portfolios of prints and a hand-press. On the journey they had no fewer than seven different chaises and drivers and each time the sixteen boxes had to be unloaded and loaded again. They arrived at Felpham near Bognor just before midnight.

But why was Blake, who had been born in London and had lived there all his life, moving to a remote Sussex seaside village at the age of 43? The answer lies in some verses he wrote a few days before leaving Lambeth:

> Away to Sweet Felpham for Heaven is there;
> The Ladder of Angels descends thro' the air;
> On the Turret its spiral does softly descend,
> Thro' the village then winds, at My Cot it does end.
>
> The Bread of sweet Thought & the Wine of Delight
> Feeds the Village of Felpham by day & by night;
> And at his own door the bless'd Hermit does stand,
> Dispensing, Unceasing, to all the whole Land.

The 'bless'd Hermit' was William Hayley, (see earlier chapter) country gentleman, poet and biographer, collector of prints and paintings, who lived alone in Turret House, Felpham. Blake earned his living by engraving and was short of work. Hayley not only wanted Blake to illustrate some of his own books but promised commissions from his many friends. He suggested that Blake move into a vacant cottage in Felpham so that they could collaborate more easily. Hayley was a kindly and benevolent soul and wanted to do what he could to help Blake, who was no doubt flattered by his attentions.

Blake was delighted with the new home; 'Our Cottage is more beautiful than I thought it, and also more convenient, for tho' small it is well-proportioned, & if I should ever build a Palace it would only be My Cottage Enlarged.' Between the cottage and the sea were cornfields now obliterated by the tide of houses spreading from nearby Bognor. From the bedroom windows he had a fine view of the sea and in later life liked to recall the white sails and shifting lights on the water.

Blake had always liked walking in the fields about Lambeth and fitted easily into country life. He was full of admiration for Sussex and Sussex people:

> Chichester is a very handsome city . . . The Country is Most Beautiful, and the People are Genuine Saxons, handsomer than the people about London . . . Sussex is certainly a happy place and Felpham in particular is the sweetest spot on earth.

Blake was now working hard on work supplied by Hayley. There were twenty heads of poets on canvas that he was painting for Hayley's library at Turret House; commissions for engravings from Hayley and from his friends; and there were other commissions from local gentry such as Lord Bathurst of Lavant and Lord Egremont of Petworth. And in all this furious activity Blake was helped by Kate his wife. Hayley described the scene; 'They have no servant – the good woman not only does all the work of the House, but she even makes the greatest part of her Husband's dress, & assists him in his art – she draws, she engraves, she sings delightfully & is so truly the Half of her good Man, that they seem animated by one Soul.'

Hayley was right; Kate was deeply devoted to a husband whose strange behaviour must often have bewildered her. He was well rewarded, for she stuck to him through hard work and poverty for 44 years and was with him when he died.

Hayley was convinced that Blake should master the art of painting miniatures and appointed himself Blake's instructor. He also thought Blake would benefit by learning Greek and in the long winter evenings Blake obediently sat by Hayley's side reading Homer.

It was an altogether improbable friendship: the fussy and conventional author of fashionable verse can have had no notion of the fiery world of the imagination in which Blake lived. What could Hayley have in common with a man who walked on the sea shore conversing with the shades of Moses, Homer, Dante and Milton?

The two men were, in fact, too disparate for the friendship to last. It was threatened from the start by the fierce independence of Blake's genius and by his intolerance of all that was merely trivial. To achieve success by money and patronage was to be untrue to those invisible powers whose servant he believed himself to be. He was, he said, 'under the direction of Messengers from Heaven, Daily & Nightly' and he wanted to get on with *their* work. In later life he would say: 'The Visions were angry with me at Felpham.' One of the savage epigrams he wrote at this time is entitled *To Hayley*:

> Thy friendship oft has made my heart to ache:
> Do be my enemy – for friendship's sake.

Blake now decided that he must return to London.

But before he could leave Blake was involved in a disturbing law suit in which Hayley, the hack poet, was to render one last service to genius. It was 1803 and it seemed likely that Napoleon Bonaparte might attempt an invasion of England. Blake got into a fierce argument with a soldier which ended with Blake bundling the soldier out of his cottage garden and down the road in front of all the villagers. To get his revenge, the soldier brought charges against Blake who was tried in January 1804 at Chichester Guildhall. The *Sussex Advertiser* reported:

> William Blake, an engraver of Felpham, was tried on a charge exhibited against him by
> two soldiers for having uttered seditious and treasonable expressions such as 'Damn the

William Blake   *Blake's Cottage, Felpham*

23

King, damn all his subjects, damn his soldiers, they are all slaves; when Bonaparte comes, it will be cut-throat for cut-throat, and the weakest must go to the wall; I will help him; etc etc.'

It was a worrying time for Blake. His defence was straight-forward; the soldiers were lying and he had the villagers to back him up. But patriotic feelings were running high and there was no telling which way judgement might go. A few years before, a Gosport bookseller was sentenced to the pillory and five years' hard labour for saying 'No George, no war'. And a Somerset basket maker was jailed for saying 'I wish success to the French'. Even though the soldiers were lying and Blake didn't say 'Damn the king' on that occasion, he was a revolutionary in politics and probably had said it at other times and places. He had written a long poem in praise of the French Revolution and another attacking George III's 'despotism'. He had been a friend of Tom Paine, author of *The Rights of Man*, and it was Blake who had advised him to flee the country to avoid arrest.

But it seems that Blake's notoriety had not yet reached the sleepy ears of Chichester. Hayley, who had stood bail for Blake at an earlier hearing, engaged a first-class barrister and himself testified in court to Blake's good character. Every time one of the soldiers lied in evidence Blake shouted out 'False!' much to the court's astonishment. *The Sussex Advertiser* ended its account of the trial:

> After a long and patient hearing he was, by the jury, acquitted; which so gratified the auditory that the court was, in defiance of all decency, thrown into an uproar by their noisy exultations.

To find Blake's Cottage in Felpham: turn into Limmer Lane opposite the Parish Church, first right into Waterloo Road, continue past the Fox Inn into Blake's Road which is opposite. The cottage is a few yards down on the left and has a blue plaque on the wall. The Fox Inn was completely rebuilt after a fire in 1946. For a note on Turret House, see the end of the chapter on William Hayley.

6. Horace Smith *(1779–1849)*   Brighton

To be a successful stockbroker and a successful poet demands a rare combination of talents. While Horace Smith worked as a lowly clerk in a City of London counting house he used his spare time to write novels about polite society. His first was published when he was only twenty-one and was followed by several others of equal dullness. It was not until he collaborated with his brother in a book of verses that Horace became the talk of London. *Rejected Addresses* included some clever parodies of well-known poets, so clever that Sir Walter Scott was convinced he had written the one alleged to be by him. The book was a great success and ran through thirty editions. It was Smith's passport to literary London. He met Keats and became a close friend of Shelley, who put him in charge of his financial affairs when he left England for Italy. Smith was to have joined him there but dallied in Versailles where he received a letter from Leigh Hunt enclosing a lock of Shelley's hair and telling of his death.

Smith made a great deal of money on the Stock Exchange and retired early to devote himself to the pleasures of writing and living. For a short while he lived in Tunbridge Wells and came across the ruins of Brambletye House in Forest Row. The romantic ruins inspired Smith to write a novel of the Civil War period. The three volumes of 1,200 pages were published in 1826. Brevity held no attraction for a man who once wrote:

> From my love of occupation I am always scribbling, often without due consideration of what I am writing, and I only wonder that so many of my frivolities have found their way into print.

Having spent many pleasant holidays at Brighton, Smith now decided to move there permanently. He bought number 10 in the newly-built Hanover Crescent which in those days backed on to open downland. Brighton was rapidly expanding. In the east the great classical squares and terraces of Kemp Town were going up in open countryside and in the west were Brunswick Square and Brunswick Terrace. Yet when Smith walked from Hanover Crescent, then on the outskirts of the town, down through Old Steine to the sea, he could describe it as 'countrified'.

Smith was a Londoner and needed the company of amusing and intelligent people. He would not have left London for a cultural desert. He had tested Brighton's society on many occasions and found it lively and welcoming. He made friends easily and attended the balls and assemblies at the Old Ship, card parties and theatres, and, if the weather was fine, promenaded on the Chain Pier or listened to the band on the Steine.

> If I mount my little white nag, and ride from Kemp Town to Brunswick Terrace I am sure

of half-a-dozen invitations to dinner. This I call enjoying life.

As an expatriate Londoner he was able to view with a sympathetic eye the crowds of Londoners who thronged Brighton in the summer months. Even before the railway came in 1841 there were fast and frequent coaches covering the fifty miles on well-surfaced roads. As many as sixteen coaches a day brought trippers from London's East End. Taking five or six hours, they stopped at The Cock at Sutton and The George in Crawley for ginger-bread and a tot of smuggled Hollands and at Stapleford Common they made a longer stop for rabbit pudding.

In 1840 he moved from Hanover Crescent to Cavendish Place, off Brighton front and there is now a plaque on number 12. His house became a magnet for the best in Brighton society and he and his charming daughters – he never mentions his wife – entertained many of the famous writers and artists of the day: Dickens, Thackeray, Ainsworth, Mark Lemon, the Revd. Sydney Smith, Tom Hood, Macaulay and the water colourist, Copley Fielding.

Horace Smith

10 Hanover Crescent, Brighton

Smith seems to have been amusing but often provocative in conversation. His political opinions were decidedly radical; no doubt they endeared him as a young man to the revolutionary Shelley. He held war to be an act of national lunacy, advocated working-class votes and condemned the Poor Law. He held that Protestants and Catholics should combine to fight against *all* religious intolerance, loathed smoking, and denounced anglers as 'fish butchers and piscatorial assassins'.

Living by the sea he had no great fondness for it and never wrote about it. He certainly never emulated that other Brightonian, Dr Johnson's friend, Mrs Thrale, who bathed in the sea before dawn in late November. Smith left us this account of his own first, timorous encounter with a bathing machine:

> Swore an oath that I would go into the sea, and got into a machine to avoid being indicted for perjury. Began to undress, and in one minute machine began to move; wondered where I was going. Fancied it was at least half a mile. Was upon the point of calling out for help, when the driver turned about. Stood trembling on the brink and at last jumped in: just time enough to be too late. Hit my elbow against the steps, and lost a ribbed cotton stocking. Felt in a glow and went home in high spirits to get another stocking. Elbow painful. Little finger asleep.

His novels are deservedly forgotten but his verse should be disinterred. Here are two splendid mock-heroic stanzas from a poem in which he bids farewell to his beloved Brighton:

> Ye circulating novelists, adieu!
> Long envious cords my black portmanteau tighten;
> Billiards, begone! avaunt, illegal loo!
> Farewell old Ocean's bauble, glittering Brighton!
>
> Long shalt thou laugh thine enemies to scorn,
> Proud as Phoenicia, queen of watering places!
> Boys yet unbreeched, and virgins yet unborn,
> On thy bleak downs shall tan their blooming faces!

Cavendish Place is off King's Road, Brighton, just west of the West Pier. Hanover Crescent is off the Lewes Road, north of St. Peter's Church.

In April 1817 Keats left his lodgings in Hampstead and journeyed by coach through
Surrey and West Sussex to Southampton. Crossing to the Isle of Wight, he stayed at
Newport, near Carisbrooke Castle, in those days romantically ivy-clad and haunted
by jackdaws. After a week on the island he suddenly left for Margate, a journey round
the coast of 150 miles. Two weeks later, still restless, he was off again. 'This evening I
go to Canterbury, having got tired of Margate; I was not right in the head when I
came.' He then left to spend Whit-week at the tiny village of Bo-Peep, near
Hastings.

Swallowed by the westwards expansion of Hastings, the village has now vanished.
Bo Peep Junction now stands on the site of the inn and there is a Bo Peep pub down on
the front. Keats stayed for no more than a week but in Hastings one day he met a
woman who was to have a profound and a lasting effect on him. The young and
beautiful Mrs Isabella Jones was summering there in the company of an old and crusty
Irish gentleman. Keats 'warmed with her and kissed her', was eager to follow this up
and wrote a poem urging her to satisfy him. But Isabella demurred and Keats had to
be content, for the nonce, with putting her into Book 2 of *Endymion* where she
appears as a nymph, rising naked from The Fishponds, a local beauty spot.

Eighteen months after returning to Hampstead, Keats met Isabella, quite by
chance, in a London street. Invited to her house, Keats thought he would improve on
Hastings; he did not want to be 'living backwards'. But he was gently repulsed: 'she
contrived to disappoint me in a way which made me feel more pleasure than a simple
kiss could do.' Isabella explained the difficulties; she knew Keats's brother George
and others of his circle and for that reason she asked Keats to keep their friendship a
close secret. Keats did as she asked, never referring to her by name in letters to
friends. History also kept their secret until, 135 years later, a Keats scholar noticed
Isabella's name in some letters to Hessey and Taylor, Keats's publishers. We now
know that there were other difficulties that Isabella did not explain to John. Taylor
was hopelessly in love with her and had written her some heart-sick sonnets that were
published anonymously in the *London Magazine*. It is probable that she was his
mistress.

Whenever Keats visited Isabella she gave him a grouse for his brother Tom who
was dying of consumption. In December 1818 the boy died, aged only nineteen.
Keats was in severe shock and during the next few weeks his friends did what they
could to distract him by taking him to theatres, concerts and once down to Crawley
Down in Sussex to see a thirty-four round barefisted boxing match. A neighbour
arranged for Keats and his friend Charles Brown to spend a few days at his father's
house in Chichester: Brown left London first, leaving Keats to follow. Keats left his
lodgings in Hampstead but stayed somewhere in London on the night of January 20th,

catching an early coach to Chichester in the morning. There are good reasons for supposing that he spent the night at Isabella Jones's house and that she was more yielding than on previous occasions. January 20th is, after all, the Eve of St Agnes, when young girls traditionally receive a vision of, if not a visit from, their lovers. Furthermore, it was Isabella who suggested that Keats should write a poem on the St Agnes theme, which he began as soon as he arrived at Chichester. Even more convincing is the poem, *Hush, hush*, probably written on the coach to Chichester, describing a secret night-time assignation with 'sweet Isabel'.

The house where Keats stayed in Chichester was in a row of tall, red brick houses built by Thomas Andrewes, a local architect, in 1780. A good number of Georgian buildings had gone up in Chichester by the time Keats got there but the medieval city, with Bishop Luffa's cathedral rising out of the clustered houses, remained unchanged. The medieval architecture of the city matched Keats's imagination, soaked as it was in gothic romance. Although he was there only a couple of days, it made a tremendous impact on his senses: 'I think it will give you the sensation of walking about an old county Town in a coolish evening' he wrote in *The Eve of St Mark*:

> All was gloom, and silent all,
> Save now and then the still foot-fall
> Of one returning homewards late,
> Past the echoing minster-gate.
> The clamorous daws, that all the day

John Keats   Eastgate Square, Chichester

Above tree-tops and towers play,
Pair by pair had gone to rest,
Each in its ancient belfry-nest,
Where asleep they fall betimes,
To music and the drowsy chimes.

The jackdaws have gone but it is still possible, 150 years later, walking in the cathedral cloisters, to recapture that tranquillity.

'I went out twice at Chichester to old dowager card parties' wrote Keats. A few days later, Keats and Brown took a post-chaise and drove to Stansted Park to attend the dedication of the Chapel. On this great occasion the park and house were open to the public and three hundred clergymen attended the service. As they had no entry tickets they had to stand or sit in the porch and stretch their necks to see anything. Keats, contemptuous of Christianity, found it 'not amusing' but in fact the rich pageantry of the scene deeply impressed him. The Chapel is a delightful piece of Regency Gothic, full of painted windows, carved woodwork and tasteful embellishments. The triple-arched windows in the nave use the arms of the Earl of Arundel, whose family, the Fitzalans, had probably built the older parts of the Chapel in the 15th century. They reappear, with much else from this Stansted visit, in several stanzas of *The Eve of St Agnes*:

A casement high and triple-arched there was,
All garlanded with carven imag'ries
Of fruits, and flowers, and bunches of knot-grass,
And diamonded with panes of quaint device,
Innumerable of stains and splendid dyes,
As are the tiger-moth's deep-damasked wings;
And in the midst, 'mong thousand heraldries,
And twilight saints, and dim emblazonings,
A shielded scutcheon blush'd with blood of queens and kings.

Brown left for London the following day but Keats was able to stay along the coast at Havant for nearly a fortnight. Here he completed *The Eve of St Agnes* which his biographer, Robert Gittings, has called, 'one of the world's great narrative poems'.

Stansted House and Chapel is open to the public for the first time in 1985, from 26th May to 15th Sept. Services are held in the Chapel every other Sunday and anyone is welcome to attend. A phone call to the Stansted Park Foundation (070 541 2265) will ensure that you arrive on the right Sunday.

The house where Keats stayed in Chichester is on the south side of Eastgate Square and has a plaque on the wall.

8. Alfred Lord Tennyson *(1809–1892)* Black Down

1850 was a good year for Tennyson: as well as marrying Emily Sellwood he was appointed Poet Laureate and published *In Memoriam*, the most prominent long poem of the Victorian age. It was an immediate success and amongst its most fervent admirers were Queen Victoria and the Prince Consort. He was well on the way to becoming an eminent Victorian, and was also becoming very wealthy.

The Tennysons' first house was a charming but impractical farmhouse at Warninglid, a few miles east of Cuckfield in Sussex. It was very old and isolated, no postman called and the doctor and butcher were seven miles away at Horsham. They moved in mid-winter and Emily was pregnant. They were both horrified to learn that the dining-room had once been a Roman Catholic chapel and that a baby had been buried on the premises. When a violent storm blew in the bedroom wall while they were in bed, they decided to leave. Alfred put Emily in a bath chair and pushed her over two miles of rough tracks to the Talbot Inn at Cuckfield.

For a short while they lived in a Georgian house in Montpelier Row at Twickenham and later bought Farringford, a large house near Freshwater on the Isle of Wight. It was surrounded by open downland with superb sea views, and Alfred was able to walk for two hours every day, a habit he kept up throughout his life. Until he was nearly eighty he never knew serious illness. Carlyle described him as 'A fine, large-featured, dim-eyed, bronze-coloured, shaggy man is Alfred, dusty, smoky, free and easy'. He drank a bottle of port every day and, said one friend, 'smokes the strongest and most stinking tobacco out of a small blackened clay pipe on an average nine hours every day'. Born in Lincolnshire, he kept a broad accent all his life and combined it with a disconcerting bluntness of speech.

He was not an easy man to live with. Undoubtedly he had his minor vexations but the domestic empire was run solely to enable him to write poetry. Emily managed the house, their two children and the servants, and was also his secretary, answering the endless stream of letters. She even made the notebooks in which he scribbed ideas for poems. But he was not a happy man: 'a congenital grumbler and hypochondriac' says one of his biographers. He was dark in temperament as well as appearance. 'We Tennysons are a black-bloodied race' he once growled. His father had been plagued with depressions and drunkenness and fits, dying heavily in debt to the local wine merchant. One of Alfred's brothers had followed his father into drunkenness, another had become an opium addict while a third spent most of his life in a lunatic asylum. Tennyson somehow managed to keep the family demons at bay.

There was a constant stream of visitors to Farringford. He had a large circle of friends and then there were always the distinguished people who came to clasp the Laureate's hand and gaze reverentially into that shaggy face. There were also less

Alfred Tennyson   *Aldworth House, Black Down*

welcome visitors – the cockneys, as Alfred called them. Crowds of holiday makers and sight-seers arrived in charabancs, peeping and prying to catch a glimpse of the Great Man mowing the lawns or pacing up and down, as a poet should, in his huge black sombrero. They even picked flowers from the garden and broke bits of stone off the walls as souvenirs. It was clearly time to go.

In 1867 Tennyson bought sixty acres of land on Black Down, a few miles south of Haslemere. The highest point on the North Downs, this sandstone hill looks out over the Weald to the distant sea. Tennyson wanted just a four-roomed cottage but with his having engaged the young and enthusiastic James Knowles as architect, it grew into what Nairn and Pevsner call 'a fussy small hotel'. It had a ballroom and an arcaded porch so that even in bad weather the poet could still take his daily walk. The cornice under the roof bore the braggart motto, in Welsh, 'The Truth against the World'. The house had the novelty of piped hot water so for some time Alfred indulged in four or five baths a day. In generous deference to his dutiful wife, the house was named Aldworth after the village in Berkshire where her ancestors lay buried.

Winters were now spent at Farringford and the rest of the year at Aldworth. For a time it afforded a refuge from the droves of admirers. Tennyson's study had a window facing south, a view described in his poem:

You came, and looked and loved the view
Long-known and loved by me,
Green Sussex fading into blue
With one gray glimpse of sea.

A track dropped four hundred feet from the house to the Weald and even in his eighties Tennyson would still go up and down it. Margot Asquith visited him in his eightieth year and remembered that 'the morning after my arrival I was invited by our host to go for a walk with him, which flattered me very much; but after walking at a great pace over rough ground for two hours I regretted my vanity'. He read his poetry to her: 'Tennyson's reading had the lilt, the tenderness and the rhythm that makes music in the soul. It was neither singing, nor chanting, nor speaking, but a subtle mixture of the three; and the effect upon me was one of haunting harmonies that left me profoundly moved.' Tennyson liked to read his poems to friends and when Edison sent him a phonograph he made a recording.

Edmund Gosse walked over from Haslemere and left us this unforgettable picture of the aged poet:

pacing up and down the lawn, a queer figure, in black broadcloth, with a soft black sombrero, and black kid gloves, shuffling along without a stick, a book under his arm . . . he has grown very queer and Rembrandtish, the skin like parchment, all the hair gone from the dome of the head, and scanty grey tufts over the ears, thin long grizzled goatee on the chin; he looks like a very old Yankee preacher.

In his last years he suffered a severe attack of rheumatic gout but he continued to write almost up to his death. The end came peacefully in October 1892. He asked them to pull up the blinds: 'I want the blinds up, I want to see the sky and the light.' Some days later a little procession set out from Aldworth. The coffin covered with wreaths and crosses of flowers sent from all over England, was put in a wagon and a coachman who had been Tennyson's faithful servant for more than thirty years, led the horse. Tennyson's son recalled:

Ourselves, the villagers, and the schoolchildren followed over the moor through our lane towards a glorious sunset, and later through Haslemere under brilliant starlight to Westminster Abbey.

Aldworth House on Black Down is completely hidden from public view by trees planted on the surrounding slopes in Tennyson's day and is strictly private. Five hundred acres of Black Down are National Trust property so everyone can enjoy that superb view of the great trough of the Weald which so entranced the poet. There is a marked footpath known as 'Tennyson's Walk'.

9. Anthony Trollope *(1815–1882)* South Harting

By including Trollope in this book it might be said that we are poaching on Essex preserves; eleven of his most prolific years were spent at Waltham Cross 'in a house in which I could entertain a few friends modestly, where we grew our cabbage and strawberries, made our own butter, and killed our own pigs'. The house is still there, opposite the Embassy Cinema in the High Street. Indulging his great passion for riding to hounds he almost came to think of himself as an Essex man. 'Essex was the chief scene of my sport, and gradually I became known there almost as well as though I had been an Essex squire.'

But Trollope had no lasting attachment to any county, unless it was to the fictional Barsetshire of his novels. His work as a travelling surveyor for the Post Office kept him on the move by horse and by train over both Ireland and England and, later, abroad. And while he travelled his eyes and his ears collected material that would reappear in his novels and travel books.

He came to live at South Harting in Sussex at the age of sixty-five, only two years before his death. His health was failing so his doctors recommended that he left London for the medicinal benefits of country air. Victorian doctors habitually sent ailing patients all over the British Isles and abroad in the conviction that a change of air would improve their health. In Trollope's case, as in so many others, the patient actually became worse. He could not sleep, his asthma was no better and he was condemned to wear an uncomfortable truss. Worst of all, he could no longer keep up his regular daily stint of writing. In his prime, when he was both a popular novelist and a senior civil servant, he paid an old groom £5 a year to wake him at five o'clock every morning with a cup of coffee. At 5.30 he was at his writing desk correcting yesterday's work and once that was done he would write until 9.30 at the rate of 250 words every quarter of an hour with his watch on the desk in front of him. After a hearty breakfast of ham, meat, fish, bacon, kidneys and eggs, he would set off for the Post Office in London. That was his regular daily routine at Waltham Cross. But those days were past now. He had retired from the Post Office and he had written his autobiography; it lay in the drawer of his desk ready to be published after his death. With his bald head, his gold-rimmed glasses, and his thick beard and his poor health, he was beginning to feel an old man. And in South Harting it was all too easy to feel old and bored. There was nothing to do there and no one to meet. It was a pleasant enough house; two large cottages had been knocked into one and a tower added with a water tank at its top. The house was celebrated locally for its futuristic plumbing – the first house in Harting to have a bathroom, all polished mahogany and polished brass taps and a bath that cleverly tilted to make emptying easier. Five acres, a cow and a few hens went with the house and there were stables for Trollope's horses. Every day he would go out riding up the track to the Downs with his niece Florence.

Hunting was out of the question now.

But it was the social life of London and the Garrick Club that he missed most of all. He had been desperately miserable at school, a feared martinet in the Post Office, and the Garrick was the only place where Trollope had learned to make friends. After leaving Waltham Cross he had moved to Montague Square, just north of Oxford Street, and every afternoon he used to ride one of his four horses down to the Garrick for tea and a rubber of whist. He would hope to see Millais there, illustrator of so many of Trollope's books; 'To see him has always been a pleasure. His voice has been a sweet sound in my ears.' They would sit and talk and smoke. Moving to Harting was a mistake. If only he could get back to London.

Sometimes, in his darkest moments, Trollope would browse amongst his five thousand books and wonder if his own were going out of fashion. Success had always meant a good deal to him and he had been shocked by the critics' severe handling of *The Prime Minister* a few years previously. On the other hand they had been

Anthony Trollope   *The Grange, South Harting*

enthusiastic about *The Duke's Children* published in the year he had moved to Harting. But there was some truth in his fears; he sniffed an air of coming disapproval and was not mistaken. After his death his sales fell sharply and remained down until the Trollope revival began in the 1930s. Trollope was always diffident about his own stature as a writer: 'I do not think it probable that my name will remain among those who in the next century will be known as the writers of English prose fiction.' He was probably almost as proud of having invented the pillar box as of writing forty-seven novels.

In 1882 Trollope shook off depression and made two visits to Ireland. He had always been a great traveller. Only ten years earlier, he and his wife Rose had gone to Australia, staying part of the time on a son's sheep farm and the rest of the time criss-crossing Australia to collect material for a travel book. (On the voyage out Trollope had stayed in his cabin and written a novel!). He had horsebacked through the West Indies, North America and South Africa writing travel books on all of them. As a young man he had been sent to Ireland by the Post Office. He had met his wife there, written his first novel and later, had written *The Warden* in Belfast. He went now to sharpen old impressions and taste again the flavours of Irish life as he had known them forty years ago. When he got back to Harting he began a new novel about Ireland, *The Land Leaguers*.

But Rose, watching his health and his spirits decline, knew that she must get him back to London. She took rooms in the Garland Hotel in Suffolk Street off Pall Mall East, a short walk from his beloved Garrick Club. For a brief while Trollope revived the old life of good food, good friends, good conversation. One evening at a party, laughing over a reading from a comic novel, Trollope slumped in his chair; a stroke had paralysed his right side. He never spoke again. For a month he lay inert in hospital before dying on December 6th, 1882. His wife survived him by an astonishing 35 years.

In a corner of South Harting church is a dusty glass case containing a small portrait of Trollope, his paperknife, penholder and letter weight. Down the main street from the church is The Ship Inn; take the turning at the side of The Ship, North Lane, which leads to Nyewood, and Trollope's house, The Grange, is on the left-hand side on the corner of the road to West Harting. The plaque on the front wall is invisible from the road but if you trespass a few paces into the drive you can see the pillared entrance to the house, two ogee windows and a tiny Victorian glasshouse on the lawn like a miniature Crystal Palace. There is also a mulberry tree, old enough to have shared its fruit with Anthony Trollope.

———————————

10. Thomas Huxley   *(1825–1895)*   Eastbourne

Thomas Huxley, the great propagandist for evolution, was not called Darwin's bulldog for nothing. He was a man of firm opinions, vigorously expressed. And whatever he did, whether dissecting a corpse or choosing a site for his retirement 'cottage', was done with masterly decision. Brighton he hated: 'Beastly Brighton' he called it. Bournemouth he liked but the air was 'too soft and moist'. Eastbourne was his choice: 'With three coats on I find the air on Beachy Head eminently refreshing' he informed a friend in November. For some time he had been flat on his back, taking digitalis for heart trouble and had gone to the Swiss Alps to recuperate. Hardly able to walk a hundred yards when he arrived, after a couple of months he was back to his customary ten miles a day and climbing 2,000 feet without difficulty. At the age of sixty-three he considered exercise the best cure for his many ills. When he returned to England he hired a house at Eastbourne, 10 Southcliff Terrace, and spent November and December looking for a suitable building plot. His brother-in-law was brought in as architect and the foundations were laid at Staveley Road in May 1889.

The work took longer than expected: 'We ought to have been in the house a month ago, but fillers, paperers, and polishers are like bugs or cockroaches, you may easily get 'em in, but getting 'em out is the deuce.' At his London home in St John's Wood he spent a fortnight sorting out his library and gave great quantities of biological books to the Royal College of Science. Huxley and his wife, Henrietta, moved in just before Christmas 1890: he called the new house Hodeslea, Anglo-Saxon for Huxley. Shortly afterwards their cook gave notice; she must have strongly disapproved of her employer's views for Huxley wrote: 'I believe she is going for no other reason than that she is afraid the house will fall on such ungodly people as we are, and involve her in the ruins.'

Huxley had worked hard all his life and saw no reason for changing his habit now that he was retired. Breakfast was always at eight o'clock followed by a pipe and one and a half hours of writing letters or editing yet another volume of his collected essays – there were nine of them in the end. Then he would potter in the garden, inspecting the plants and noting their progress or decline and work again in his book-crammed study until lunch. At half-past-two he would set out for his walk across the Downs; the air on Beachy Head, 560 feet up, was an unfailing tonic. After his walk a cup of tea was followed by more study until dinner at seven. In the evening he would read and smoke his pipe until bed at midnight.

Huxley became a keen gardener at Eastbourne. Primarily a zoologist, he acquired a passion for gentians in the Alps and wrote a scientific paper comparing the various species. The alpine saxifrage was another of his favourites and he built a rock garden at Hodeslea to accommodate them. Growing creepers on the house walls was another pleasure. His gardener was sceptical of Huxley's efforts: 'Books? They'll say anything in them books!' He especially deplored Huxley's fondness for watering the garden with a hosepipe.

Huxley had retired from his presidency of the Royal Society, from his professorship at South Kensington and from his government work but he had never retired from the intellectual arena. Ever since 1859 when he had reviewed Darwin's *Origin of Species* for *The Times*, Huxley had been a gladiator in the great Victorian contest between theology and evolution. Thirty years of lecturing, writing and campaigning had given him an addiction to controversy. A new controversy always improved his health, even if it worsened his temper. Depressions would vanish, his mental engine would slip into top gear and he would stride about the house, slamming doors and denouncing his opponent. When Gladstone, one of his old sparring partners, published *Impregnable Rock of Holy Scripture* in 1890, the temptation was irresistible. And no sooner had Huxley engaged with Gladstone than he was

Thomas Huxley

Hodeslea, Staveley Road, Eastbourne

drawn into a furious controversy about the Salvation Army. A woman who was about to donate £1,000 to its funds had asked Huxley his opinion: after investigating the Army he wrote a series of letters to *The Times* warning its readers of the grave danger to the nation from the Sally Ann's excessively enthusiastic religion. He wrote to a friend: 'This old dog has never let go after fixing his teeth into anything or anybody and he is not going to begin now.' It was six months before these controversies died down. Promising that he was 'going to be good – till next time', Huxley admitted, 'but in truth I am as sick of controversy as a confectioner's boy of tarts'. Perhaps he was, but he was unable to break the habit and a year later his name was reappearing in the letter columns of *The Times*.

Visits to London became increasingly exhausting; 'three days of London bowls me over' and there was the risk of catching influenza from London's fogs. But some visits were unavoidable. In 1893 he gave a lecture at Oxford's Sheldonian Theatre on 'Evolution and Ethics'. For some time he had been fighting a heavy cold which had produced pimples on his nose and reduced his voice to a whisper. The Sheldonian was packed to the doors and there were shouts of 'speak up' from those who had come to hear Darwin's bulldog for what many must have suspected was the last time. Few of those present could have heard all he said but perhaps the sight of that square and resolute head with the great mane of swept-back hair was enough. He had lived long enough to become a legend.

Early in 1895, the politician A.J. Balfour published a book called *The Foundation of Belief* in which, without actually naming Huxley, he made lethal criticisms of Huxley's position. Huxley was stung to retaliate and planned a two-part article refuting Balfour. The first part was published but before he could complete the second an influenza epidemic swept Eastbourne and he, his wife and one of their maids were all laid low. For four months he struggled against flu and bronchitis. When he recovered he was found to have advanced heart and kidney disease. His son, Leonard, remembered him, 'browned with the endless sunshine of the 1895 summer as he sat every day in the verandah. When I asked him how he was he said, "A mere carcass which has to be tended by other people"'.

He was buried in Finchley Cemetery, London, beside his four-year old son Noel. An oak tree, which had been a sapling when Noel was buried beneath it thirty-five years before, was now a strong young tree.

'Hodeslea' is at the corner of Staveley and Buxton Roads at the western end of Eastbourne. There is a plaque on the wall. Huxley's apsidal library with its stained glass windows can be seen from the outside.

---

11. Augustus Hare *(1834–1903)* Herstmonceux &
Ore

Augustus Hare was born in Rome and his parents were 'greatly annoyed at the birth of another child and beyond measure disgusted that it was another son'. When Aunt Maria, recently widowed, offered to adopt Augustus, they readily agreed and reminded her that 'if anyone else would like one, would you kindly recollect that we have others'. For the rest of his life Augustus regarded Maria as his mother and they were devoted to each other.

Aunt Maria lived in the Lime, an old white gabled house with clustered chimneys in Herstmonceux, Sussex. In the nearby barn corn was still threshed with a flail after being reaped with sickle or scythe: the ox had not yet been replaced by the farmhorse. In a courtyard next to the house they kept silver pheasants. But across the boy's childhood years fell the dark shadow of Uncle Julius, rector of Herstmonceux, and his wife Esther, sister of the Revd. F.D. Maurice, spiritual leader of the Christian Socialist Movement. The uncle was bad enough, beating the boy with a horse whip for the most trivial faults but his wife had an altogether more sophisticated taste in cruelty: she set herself to deprive him of every small pleasure in life, from reading to eating lollipops. When she found he had a pet cat she ordered a servant to hang it. She was devoutly religious and exercised an evil influence on Aunt Maria.

In these circumstances it was a relief to be sent to Harrow to endure the customary fagging and floggings. Oxford was more civilised with the great Benjamin Jowett, Master of Balliol, as his tutor. It was while at Oxford that Augustus had his first taste of foreign travel: he and a young poet took £25 each and toured France and Germany for six weeks. Travel was to become an addiction and writing tourist guides an occupation. This is also when he began cultivating his amazingly wide circle of friends and relatives. His natural mother was descended – as is the present Queen Mother – from the 8th Earl of Strathmore and Aunt Maria, by marriage, could boast of a bishop or two. By combining both family trees Augustus had at his disposal some useful connections in church, county and aristocracy.

There followed a long series of guides for English tourists to Paris, Rome, Venice, Florence, the regions of Italy and France, Spain, Holland, Scandinavia and even Russia. And all his guides were illustrated with engravings from his own charming sketches and water-colours. His industry was immense. He did a great deal of reading in several languages and quoted so liberally from other writers that one of them accused him of 'barefaced and wholesale robbery'. Murray's, publishers of a rival series of guides, took legal action against Hare. He survived it all with an air of injured innocence which must have been galling to his critics since they undoubtedly had grounds for complaint. When his books were spitefully reviewed he consoled himself with the improving thought that 'bad reviews are capital teachers of humility'.

Augustus Hare   *Holmhurst, Ore*

In 1861 he and his 'mother' left Herstmonceux and bought Holmhurst with thirty-six acres of land at Ore near Hastings. This was to be Hare's home for the rest of his life. He never seems to have given any serious thought to marriage. He had a pattern of work and travel which he found completely satisfying. Throughout the winter he would be abroad collecting material and on his return he would spend the rest of the year writing it up in his beloved Holmhurst.

Hare filled Holmhurst with antiquarian bits and pieces picked up here and there in his travels. In a London cellar he paid £4 for two statues from the ancient church of All Hallows, Barking; from Baynard's Castle in Surrey came carved beams, oak panels from Winchelsea Church and coloured windows from Herstmonceux Castle. He was specially proud of discovering in a London junk yard the statue of Queen Anne which once stood outside St Paul's Cathedral – the present one is a copy. Weighing four tons the Queen arrived by train in Sussex and was hauled to Holmhurst by twenty-eight horses.

On all his travels Hare methodically kept a journal which he later used, together with his long letters to his mother, to write his *Story of My Life*. The first three volumes came out in 1896, followed by another three in 1900. He was working on a further instalment when he died. It is probably the longest autobiography in the language – about three-quarters of a million words. The critics complained of the book's inordinate length but Hare ignored them: he wrote on the assumption that you cannot have too much of a good thing. The book records in great detail all his many journeys and the people he met and the conversations he had. He found good stories irresistible and wrote them all down, probably adding a few touches of colour to improve them. He was on friendly terms with most prominent people in church and politics. He breakfasted on strawberries with Gladstone, stayed with a titled relative in a haunted castle in Scotland and, when the Archbishop of Canterbury died, he could pride himself on having had an 'ever-kind welcome' from the last *five* archbishops.

At the age of sixty-two even Hare was tiring of foreign travel. 'Is it a sign of old age coming on when one has a distaste for leaving home? I simply hate it.' He was comfortable at Holmhurst with his devoted servants, his black spitz dog and the flowering gardens. In 1898 the gardens were altered to an Italian design copied from his sketchbooks. A stone terrace was built and a massive classical archway with AVE on one side to welcome the guest and VALE on the other to speed his parting. Cypresses were planted and vases and obelisks carefully sited.

> As I write this, and look from my window across the tiny terrace with its brilliant flowers to the oakwoods, golden in the autumn sunset, and the blue sea beyond, with the craggy mass of Hastings Castle rising up against it, I feel that there are few places more lovely than Holmhurst.

His other two handbooks on English counties belong to these later years; Sussex published in 1894 and Shropshire in 1898. The dull antiquarian lore is occasionally lit by flashes of exasperation: Worthing is 'a very ugly, uninteresting place', Brighton Pavilion 'a foolish Chinese palace', and of a stained glass window in Chichester Cathedral he says; 'its execrable glass, executed in Lorraine, was at Metz during the siege, and unfortunately not destroyed there'. The Sussex book must have sold well for a second edition was published two years later.

The Lime (now Lime Park) is much altered since Hare's day, but still has a magnificent setting. A look at the house is worth combining with a visit to Herstmonceux Castle, one mile away. Turn south off the A271 at the signpost to the castle. Lime Park is opposite the 'Welcome Stranger' pub.

Although Hare gave his address as Ore, Holmhurst is in fact in Baldslow. It is now known as Holmhurst St. Mary and is on the south side of the B2093 which leads to Ore, opposite the Beaulieu Farm Dairy. It is run as a conference centre by Anglican sisters of the Community of the Holy Family. Hare's Italian terrace and the Ave-Vale arch survive, Queen Anne still stands on her massive plinth and Hare's favourite view of the distant sea from the terrace is still unspoilt. Appointments to view Holmhurst can be made by phoning Reverend Mother Sister Joan at Hastings (0424) 754000.

12. W.H. Hudson *(1841–1922)*

William Hudson was 33 years old when he left Argentina where he had been brought up and sailed for England. He had no very clear idea of what he would do here. In South America at the age of six he had galloped bare-back across the the pampas: at ten he was shooting wild-duck with an old fowling-piece. For years he helped his father on the cattle ranch and all the time he was watching birds and insects and animals and carefully recording what he saw in notebooks.

His obsession with birds brought him work as a collector for natural museums. He shot hundreds of rare birds and dispatched abroad the neatly labelled skins with vivid and exact descriptions of the bird's behaviour. Many of these notes were published by the Zoological Society of London. Three new bird species that he discovered were named after him. But the work was so badly paid that it hardly covered the cost of the ammunition and he was forced to give it up. He had, it is true, achieved a reputation as a field naturalist of some distinction but he felt little in common with the scientists who bought his skins.

Two years after coming to England he married. His wife was an unsuccessful concert soprano reduced to giving music lessons to unpromising pupils.

> I was never in love with my wife nor she with me. I married her because her voice moved me as no singing voice had ever done before.

She remained devoted to him through forty-five years of married life.

Emily inherited Tower House in St Luke's Road, Westbourne Park, London, which they kept for the rest of their lives: it is still standing and bears a commemorative plaque. The house was heavily mortgaged so they lived in the attic and let the lower floors. They were painfully poor for many years: 'One week we lived on a tin of cocoa and milk' wrote Hudson. He longed to spend days walking in the country but shortage of money limited these expeditions to two or three a year. For the rest of the time he had to satisfy his hunger for birds and greenery in London's parks. He was a painstakingly slow writer and his work met with repeated rejections. London became a prison and he bitterly regretted leaving the pampas where, for so many years, he had lived with the gauchos and slept in his poncho under the stars.

When his novel *The Purple Land* was accepted by a publisher he thought he had broken through; he was mistaken. It was so savaged by the critics that neither publisher nor author made a penny out of it. He had to wait until seven years later when *The Naturalist in La Plata* appeared to get the acclaim he deserved. It was hailed as a masterpiece; but masterpieces are often less financially rewarding than pot-boilers and Emily and William remained hard-up until friends managed to get him a Civil List pension of £150 a year.

Hudson now began making visits to Shoreham in Sussex where he stayed with artist friends. On arriving, he would go straight to the shingle beach – now ribboned with smart bungalows – and celebrate his return to the wilderness of nature by drinking a handful of sea-water. In 1899 Hudson spent most of his time exploring the Sussex downs and writing *Nature in Downland*. The first chapter was written in the house at Goring where, only a few years before, the young Richard Jefferies had died. Searching for the house Hudson had a remarkable experience:

> My mind was full of sadness, when, hearing the crunching of gravel beneath other feet than my own, I suddenly looked up, and behold, there before me stood the man himself, back on earth in the guise of a tramp! It was a most extraordinary coincidence that at such a moment I should have come face to face with a poor outcast and wanderer who had Jefferies' countenance as I knew it from portraits and descriptions. I was startled at the expression, the unmistakable stamp of a misery that was anguish and near to despair and insanity.

The footpath where this meeting took place leads westwards out of Goring churchyard. (St. Mary's Church, at the west end of Goring Road.)

Hudson's book should not be missed by anyone who walks the Sussex downs: the ordinary walker would need several lifetimes to discover for himself all the tiny details of plant, insect and bird life that are between its covers. It is one of those rare books that traps the subtle spirit of a place and holds it for us to wonder at. He gives his readers new eyes, new ears, and a new sensitivity. And when he does instruct he is never pedantic. The downs today are much the same as when Hudson walked them. The only marked differences are that tractors have replaced the teams of six long-horned oxen and sheep and shepherds have all but disappeared. That is something Hudson did not foresee: 'The solitary shepherd with his dog at his feet will doubtless stand watching his flock on the hillside for some thousands of years to come.' Nor could he have foreseen that the Saxon type that he met in all Sussex villages with 'round, rosy face, steady, sometimes hard blue eyes, and light brown hair' would be mongrelised to the point of extinction by London's overspill. The trapping of skylarks and wheatears for food was common on the downs in Hudson's day and he was actively campaigning for laws to prevent it. Nothing made him more angry than this trade in wild birds. The shepherds who trapped them to sell to the hotels in Brighton and Eastbourne were trying to augment their disgracefully low wages of 12/6d a week. It was inconsistent of Hudson, who had once shot birds for a living, to condemn the shepherds.

Although Hudson never earned much money from his books he was now writing with greater ease and publishers were ready to take his work. There is no doubt that Hudson would have left London to live in the country but Emily was attached to Tower House and would not leave. Friends were appalled to find the great naturalist living in the gloomy house in the down-at-heel bed-sit territory of West London. But in later years Hudson's tramping jaunts were more prolonged and then in 1913 Emily became seriously ill. It was decided to move her to a comfortable boarding house in

W.H. Hudson

Huntingdon House, Bedford Row, Worthing

Park Road, Worthing. Hudson wrote to Emily every few days and sometimes stayed at the boarding house, taking her down to the sea in a wheel chair. When the boarding house was full he would stay at Huntingdon House, 8 Bedford Row, a bow-fronted Regency terrace off the sea-front that now has a pleasantly faded elegance. Worthing is an inoffensive resort but it inspired Hudson with violently hostile feelings:

> I hate the place and have never yet met anyone in it who has been of use to me. It is talk, talk, talk, but never a gleam of an original or fresh remark or view of anything that does not come out of a book or newspaper

Emily never returned to London. After moving to 3 Woodlea Road, Worthing, she died in 1921 and was buried in the nearby Broadwater Cemetery. Hudson had arranged for them to be buried together at Broadwater as Richard Jefferies was also there. When death came, eighteen months later, it came quietly and his body was brought down from Tower House to lie with hers. On the kerb around the grave are these words: 'He loved birds and green places and the wind on the heath, and saw the brightness of the skirts of God.' Wild briar roses were planted at the four corners of the grave which still flower today.

Broadwater Cemetery is in South Farm Road, a turning off the A24 on the northern fringe of Worthing. Go in at the main entrance gates, turn immediately right and walk until you come to the far boundary fence. Turn left and Hudson's grave is against the fence under a row of pine trees.

The boarding house in Park Road has been demolished but Bedford Row is still there.

Richard Jefferies' house in Goring-by-Sea can be visited; for details see list of writers at the end of the book.

13. Henry James *(1843–1916)* Rye

I have been to the South, the far end of Florida etc – but I prefer the far end of Sussex! In the heart of the orange groves I yearned for the shade of the old Lamb House mulberry tree.

Before coming to Sussex, Henry James had spent twenty-two years in London, schooling himself in the manners and conversation of upper-class society. The mantelpiece of his Kensington flat was always crowded with invitations to dinner and weekends in country houses. In his ambition to become more English than the English he had even removed all trace of his American accent. But cultivating success in polite society meant that James was spending less time writing and reading and he began to look about for a country retreat. He had once seen a drawing of Lamb House and in 1896 he visited Rye to see it in the flesh. Walking up the grass-grown cobbled street and catching his first sight of the panelled and brass-knockered front door framed by the Georgian windows, he lost his heart to it. After making, as he put it, 'sheep's eyes at Lamb House', he called at the local ironmonger's shop to make some inquiries, arranging with the shopkeeper to let him know if the house ever fell vacant. It was a long shot, but the following year the ironmonger wrote saying that Lamb House was unexpectedly vacant and could be rented. James went down to Rye at once and quickly arranged the terms.

There was work to be done before James could move in: oak panelling that had been papered over had to be stripped and repainted, curtaining had to be chosen and made up and a bath with running water was installed. A telephone was fitted in a small room off the hall and gas lighting in the kitchen; James insisted on keeping oil lamps in the rest of the house and servants would sometimes find him asleep over his writing desk, his face covered in lamp black! When he had bought 'a sufficient quantity of ancient mahogany-and-brass odds and ends' to add to the furnishings, James moved in with his four servants, his Dachshund bitch Tosca and his bicycle. His collection of five thousand books followed later.

After so many years in the fog and grime of Victorian London, James found both house and garden an inexhaustible delight. He liked to think that George the First had spent four nights in the house when his ship grounded on the nearby Camber Sands. The garden was surrounded by an old brick wall supporting grapes, apricots, pears and figs. Homesick on a visit to America, James once said he would gladly trade the whole State of Connecticut for 'the battered old purple wall of poor dear little Lamb House garden'. There was a fine old mulberry tree on the lawn and to look after the garden for twenty-two shillings a week was George Gammon who lived in a cottage at the end of the garden.

It was James's inflexible habit to write from 9.30 to 1.30 every morning and no

Henry James   *Lamb House, Rye*

visitors were allowed to interrupt him. In the summer he worked in the wistaria-hung Garden Room whose large bow-window overlooked the cobbled street; the room was completely demolished by a German bomb in 1940. The rest of the year he withdrew to the Green Room on the first floor of the house. Pacing incessantly up and down he dictated to his secretary/typist. Occasionally he would pause to spell a word or else, half-way through one of his notoriously long, labyrinthine sentences he would lose his way and ask her to read it back to him. He found the metallic click of a Remington typewriter specially stimulating and would have no other machine used.

In the afternoon he went out for rides on his bicycle or for walks. In his first summer at Rye he cycled ten miles across the marshes to visit H.G. Wells who was seriously ill in New Romney. When Wells recovered enough to visit Lamb House he noticed on a hall table,

> a number of caps and hats, each with is appropriate gloves and sticks, a tweed cap and a stout stick for the Marsh, a soft comfortable deerstalker if he were to turn aside to the Golf Club, a light-brown felt hat and a cane for a morning walk down to the Harbour, a grey felt hat with a black band and a gold-headed cane of greater importance, if afternoon calling in the town were afoot.

Rye was a very small community of retired people in those days and James knew everyone from the mayor to the fishmonger. His manner of talking to shop assistants or passers-by was no different to his style of writing, the long sentences would uncoil like the tentacles of an octopus, reaching out in all directions, exploring every ramification of even so apparently simple an act as buying a packet of envelopes. It is not surprising that most people were baffled by Mr James though some kept by them his often strange utterances for the rest of their days. Stopping once to give some children a few pennies for sweets, he began to address them with scholarly seriousness on which were the best sweets to buy and which was the best shop to buy them in. The children were so over-awed by this performance that they ran away in terror, forgetting even to take the pennies. James was quite at a loss to understand their behaviour.

Stories of his harmless eccentricities added to the common fund of Rye gossip. His cook liked to tell how once she stopped him in Rye to tell him of some small domestic matter and he was unable to remember who she was. He would often stop on his walks through the town, lost in thought, with one thumb in his watch-chain. He was a kind man to all in need; many writers who were hard-up benefited from his generosity and tramps knew that bread and cheese could always be had at Lamb House.

James loved visitors and would always press them to stay overnight. Edith Wharton the American novelist was a close friend and visited often. A steady stream of famous writers made their way to the green front door with the brass knocker: Wells, Conrad, Kipling, Chesterton, Edmund Gosse, Stephen Crane, Max Beerbohm, Rupert Brooke.

Towards the end of his life the winters at Rye were too windy and cold for James and he would withdraw to the Reform Club in Pall Mall or his flat in Carlyle Mansions, Chelsea. He was troubled by angina and depression probably brought on by the failure of the Collected Edition of his novels. His books had never sold well; 'I am past all praying for . . . I remain at my age, and after my long career, utterly, insurmountably, unsaleable.' The Great War induced an almost jingoistic patriotism in James and he became a naturalised British subject. In October 1915 he made what was to be his last visit to Lamb House and found that the old mulberry tree had been blown down in a gale. Returning to London he had two severe strokes. Once, in his delirium, he asked to be moved back to his 'dear little house' in Rye. He died a few weeks later. In his will he left legacies of £100 to each of his servants and to George Gammon his gardener. Lamb House he left to his nephew who later presented it to the National Trust.

 Lamb House is in West Street, Rye, facing the west end of the church, and is well worth visiting. The walled garden, the staircase hall, the morning room, dining room and study on the ground floor are all on view.

Open: April to end October. Wednesday and Saturday only. 2pm–6pm (last admission 5.30pm). Admission charge.

14. Francis Thompson   *(1859–1907)*   Storrington

Francis Thompson knew Sussex as a kind of convalescent ward to which friends brought him when it seemed as if London and opium would destroy him. It was hoped that in the peace of the countryside and in the care of those who loved him his mind and body would mend. For a time it did – a brief time, but long enough for him to write his poems.

He was born into a devout Catholic family in Lancashire. His father was a doctor and sent his son to medical school but dissecting and the sight of blood repelled Francis. Instead of attending lectures he spent his time in libraries reading and writing poetry. Repeatedly he failed his exams. He had also to conceal from his parents the fact that he had become an opium addict. In addition to being prescribed it during a bout of fever, his mother had given him a copy of De Quincey's *Confessions of an English Opium Eater* – a fateful gift. Abandoning medicine, he tried selling encyclopedias and in desperation offered himself to the army but was rejected on medical grounds. He was twenty-six when he suddenly left home for London.

He arrived with a copy of Blake's poems in one pocket and Aeschylus in the other: all his other precious books he had sold to buy laudanum. He worked for a time as a bookseller's messenger. When he lost the job he took to reading in Guildhall Library. But lack of money had forced him to sleep in doss-houses and he was now so umkempt that a policeman barred him from going into the library. Employers turned him away on sight and he was reduced to begging.

From doss-house beds at a shilling a night he took to sleeping on the Embankment and under the Arches at Charing Cross. One week he earned only sixpence, for holding a horse's head. He would run behind hansom cabs to earn a few pence unloading the luggage when they stopped. He tried his hand as a boot-black and at selling matches in the gutter. Lord Rothschild once gave him a florin. Some of his small earnings were always spent at the chemist's on the bottles of laudanum that would bring release from the pain of cold, hunger and desolation of spirit.

Somehow he still managed to write, in pencil and on scraps of grimy paper. He slipped some of his work through the letter box of *Merry England*, a Catholic journal, asking for a reply to be sent to the Charing Cross Post Office. As the weeks passed and none came his despair deepened. He spent his remaining pence on one large dose of laudanum. He had swallowed half of it when Chatterton, the poet who killed himself in London at the age of eighteen, appeared to him in a vision forbidding him to take the rest.

Some months later the editor, Wilfred Meynell, belatedly replied and invited Thompson to his office:

> When he came into the room he half opened the door and then retreated and did so twice before he got courage to come inside. He was in rags, his feet, without stockings, showing

through his boots, his coat torn, and no shirt. He seemed in the last stage of physical collapse.

Meynell set himself to rescue Thompson from the streets and from the grip of opium. He started publishing Thompson's poetry in his journal and he and his wife, Alice, opened their home to him and became his closest friends.

Thompson was at last persuaded to try to break his addiction by staying at the White Canons monastery, at Storrington in Sussex. There, in the quiet of the country, he began to struggle out of an old life into a new. He wrote to Meynell: 'If I have indeed begun to acquire the power of working in the teeth of nerves and mood and bilious melancholy, then the fight is half fought. And I think I have.' Spending his days half writing and half walking he wrote asking Meynell for books and boots. The effect of abstaining from opium was to release a stream of fine poetry that brought the Meynells down from London by train to congratulate him. The poem that most impressed them was *Ode to the Setting Sun*, inspired by a huge twelve-foot high

Francis Thompson

White Canons Monastery, Storrington

wooden crucifix that stood in the monastery grounds and can still be seen in the monastery cloister.

After a year at Storrington he was convinced he had broken his addiction: now he needed literary work and that could only be had in London. In February 1890 he took leave of the village he had come to love.

Back in London he lived in lodgings near the Meynells' house in Bayswater and worked hard at journalism and poetry: *The Hound of Heaven* was written about this time. But the telltale signs of drug-taking reappeared; the flushed face, the missed appointments, petulance over trifles, the pedantic discussion of trivialities. Meynell now introduced him to the Franciscan friars who had friaries in Flintshire and at Crawley in Sussex. Thompson made frequent visits to both and made friends of several of the monks. His last visit to Crawley was towards the end of his life in 1906. He lodged near the friary at 11 Victoria Road and it was a cold January when he wrote to Meynell –

> I just manage to get on when it's not cold, and have a horrible time when it is. I get better food than I ever had in lodgings since Storrington, and keep shut up in a nice warm room, or else – but for these things – I should go to pieces.

He returned to London in the summer but Meynell was so disturbed by his painfully thin appearance that he arranged for him to stay on Wilfred Blunt's estate, Newbuildings Place, at Southwater, near Horsham. Blunt was a traveller and writer who bred Arab horses, kept peacocks for eating and rode around his estate in Bedouin robes. It was a long and beautiful summer but Thompson was not aware of it. He took his regular doses of laudanum and at night lay propped on his pillows with his prayer book in his hand. He returned to London in October weaker than he went. He confided to Meynell that he was dying of laudanum poisoning: in fact he was dying of tuberculosis and for the past two years it was only the laudanum that kept him going. He was a living skeleton weighing only five stones. He was moved to hospital and was nursed devotedly by a nun for a fortnight before he died at dawn on November 13th, 1907. His grave is in St Mary's Cemetery, Kensal Green.

At his death he was still wearing the holy medal round his neck that he had worn all his life. As for other possessions, his years as a vagrant in London had taught him the vanity of worldly goods; he desired none and kept none. He left only a tin box of refuse – pipes that would not draw, a spirit lamp without a wick, unopened letters, pens that would not write.

The White Canons are still at Storrington: turn south off the High Street into Church Street and right into School Lane. The Franciscans left Crawley in 1980 and the friary buildings are due to be demolished and the land sold. Crawley has one surviving link with Francis Thompson – the house at 11 Victoria Road.

15. Sir Arthur Conan Doyle   *(1859–1930)*   Crowborough

Doyle began life as a doctor in the neighbouring county of Hampshire. At first he had small success as a doctor and it was while waiting for patients that he first tried his hand at writing stories. It was here that he created Sherlock Holmes – Sherringford Holmes as he was first called. *The Study in Scarlet*, in which the great detective made his first appearance, was sold outright by Doyle for only £25.

He left Southsea after eight years and after a failed attempt to set up as an eye-specialist in London he finally abandoned medicine for a career as an author. Holmes stories were by now appearing regularly in the *Strand* magazine and the British reading public was under the spell of the omniscient investigator. Yet Doyle himself was irritated by the easy success of the Holmes stories and would have preferred to be celebrated for historical novels like *The White Company* into which he put years of painstaking research.

During the Boer War Doyle took his butler with him and volunteered to serve in a field hospital. He helped fight an epidemic of enteric fever which wiped out thousands of British soldiers. In what little spare time he had he wrote a history of the War which he finished and had published before the War was officially over. He believed that Britain's part in the War was just and he was infuriated by journalists like W.T. Stead who did their best to disparage Britain. Doyle began a one-man campaign to justify Britain's case. He published a booklet on the War that sold 300,000 copies in six weeks.

In 1897 Doyle, who by then had been married for 12 years, fell desperately in love with a girl who was fourteen years younger than himself. Doyle's wife had recently become ill with consumption and was not expected to live for long. In fact she survived for another nine years. During that time Doyle carried on a secret love affair with Jean Lecky. His wife remained ignorant of it but some of Doyle's Catholic relatives noticed what was going on and there were furious arguments in which Doyle defended the deceit on the shaky grounds that the affair was purely Platonic.

Doyle married Jean Lecky in the year following his wife's death and they moved into Windlesham Manor, the large, five-gabled house in Crowborough with its wide views across the Sussex Downs. Here during the Great War, walking in his rose garden in the quiet of the early morning, Doyle wrote of hearing 'very faint and very far, and yet with a deep throb in it', the thunder of the guns on the Western Front. He was one of the first to organise a local force of volunteer Home Guards, taking the men camping on the Downs. As with everything else that Doyle did it was tackled with such energy that the War Office, thoroughly alarmed, asked him to disband it.

At weekends the house was full of famous guests from London. A vast billiard room ran the full width of the house. Here, while Jean played her grand piano under the ornamental palm trees, Doyle relaxed at one of his favourite games. He was always a great sportsman; he had made a century in his first appearance at Lord's and had once bowled out W.G. Grace. He was an amateur boxing heavy-weight and a crack shot who always kept a loaded pistol in his desk drawer. When he took his first wife to Switzerland for her health he became one of a handful of mad Englishmen who introduced skiing into that country.

Both as a man and as a writer Doyle was remarkably insensitive to nature – the rare descriptive passages in his books are dull and conventional. His novel *Rodney Stone*, about prize-fighting in the nineteenth-century, is set in Sussex villages yet ignores the presence of the Downs. But it is worth reading for the picture it gives of the bare-knuckle pugilists whose marathon bouts attracted thousands of spectators. In Doyle's

Sir Arthur Conan Doyle

Windlesham Manor, Crowborough

book Belcher trains Boy Jim for his fight with Crab Wilson at the famous George Inn at Crawley, one of the few pubs that has a gallows sign stretching right across the road. The nearby Crawley Downs and Copthorne Common were the scenes of many historic fights in Regency days. Crawley being on the main London to Brighton road, the Prince Regent and his cronies were often amongst the crowds.

Doyle's talents were admirably suited to the Holmes stories but, like so many writers of modest talents, he believed himself destined for higher things. The success of the Holmes stories, he thought, distracted the public's attention from his really important work, the historical novels. He therefore decided to get rid of the great detective, arranging for him and the infamous Dr. Moriarty to fall to their deaths from the Reichenbach Falls, near Interlaken in Switzerland. Shortly afterwards, Doyle was offered 30,000 dollars by a American publisher for six new Holmes stories. Although now a very wealthy man with no real need for the money, he found the offer irresistible; the great detective was resurrected and his 'death' clumsily explained away.

Doyle was an incurable campaigner, a knight-errant in quest of wrongs to be righted. Often he would give money as well as his pen to causes he took up. After his booklet on the Boer War he published another entitled *The Crime of the Congo* attacking King Leopold of Belgium for the alleged cruelty of Belgians on their rubber plantations. A few years later he was working with the Divorce Reform Union and speaking on the same platform as George Bernard Shaw in favour of Home Rule for Ireland.

But the cause that Doyle came to believe in most fervently was Spiritualism. Since his early days at Southsea he had been interested enough to attend seances but he was never really convinced. During the Great War, his own son Malcolm was killed and he received a 'message' from him. He never revealed the message except to say that it was so personal that he could not doubt that it was genuine. To Doyle it was the objective proof for which he had waited for thirty years. His last eleven years were spent in an energetic campaign to convince the rest of mankind of the truth of his new creed. After publishing *The New Revelation* he did lecture tours of Africa and Australia and two of the USA. Collapsing on a Scandinavian tour he ignored the warnings of doctors and died in 1930. He was buried in the grounds of his Sussex home near the garden hut. On a headstone of English oak were inscribed the words: 'Steel true, blade straight.'

Windlesham Manor, now a private home for elderly people, is on the outskirts of Crowborough on a road called Sheep Plain which turns off the A26 at the signpost to Jarvis Brook. The road goes across the golf course on Crowborough Common and the house is the first on the left. There is a plaque beside the front door. The house in Southsea where Doyle had his doctor's practice was bombed in the last war but there is a plaque on the wall of the flats which have replaced it.

16. Rudyard Kipling *(1865–1936)* Rottingdean & Burwash

In 1891 Kipling returned from his last visit to India, married Carrie an American girl, and spent the next four years in America. When they came back to England they had two daughters and were looking for a permanent home. For a few months they lived in a house near Torquay but Kipling hated the stuffy town.

> Torquay is such a place as I do desire acutely to upset by dancing through with nothing on but my spectacles.

The Kiplings left when Rudyard's uncle, Burne-Jones the painter, invited them to share North End House, his summer retreat at Rottingdean near Brighton. This house was on one side of the village green while on another was *The Dene* where the Ridsdales lived; their daughter married Stanley Baldwin, Rudyard's cousin and the future Prime Minister. On the third side was The Elms which the Kiplings moved into later that year. As Kipling said: 'You could throw a cricket ball from any one house to another.'

They were happy days at first. Kipling later recalled the hot August days,

> packing farm-carts filled with mixed babies – Stanley Baldwin's and ours – and despatching them into the safe, clean heart of the motherly Downs for jam-smeared picnics.

Angela Thirkell, the novelist, was a grand-daughter of Burne-Jones and remembered staying as a child at North End House and playing Roundheads and Cavaliers with Cousin Ruddy and his two girls. And she recalled the fun of hearing Ruddy read the *Just-So Stories* in his 'deep, unhesitating voice'.

They had moved to Rottingdean in 1897, the year of the Queen's Diamond Jubilee. Kipling was 32 and at the height of his fame. He wrote a poem on the Jubilee but tossed it into the waste paper basket. A friend rescued it and told him it was too good to throw away. Later that day it was sent to *The Times* newspaper which published it under the title 'Recessional'. It became famous as a hymn sung on memorial occasions and warned against the very jingoistic pride which he was accused of by ignorant critics.

After Carrie had given birth to a son, John, they moved into The Elms, renting it for three guineas a week. Kipling's study was on the ground floor, just inside the entrance on the right. Here he finished *Stalky & Co*, the *Just-So Stories and Kim*.

The following year came another voyage. Carrie wanted to visit her family again in America but it was mid-winter and Kipling, with some reluctance, agreed. It was a bad crossing and when they docked at New York the whole family was ill. The two girls had whooping-cough and Kipling an inflamed lung. Kipling's condition worsened: he was too ill to be told that Josephine, his beloved eight-year old daughter, had died. In later life his other daughter Elsie wrote: 'His life was never the same after her death; a light had gone out that could never be rekindled.'

Back in Rottingdean, in addition to their personal sorrow, there was the irritating curiosity of sightseers. The horse-drawn bus from Brighton would draw up against the high flint wall that surrounded Kipling's garden. Standing on the top the trippers could stare down on the family having tea on the lawn. Some even got into the garden. One woman stared in at Kipling's study window and when he drew the blind she exclaimed 'How rude!' Small cheques signed by Kipling for local tradesmen were never cashed since they could be sold to collectors for more than their face value.

The nuisance of sight-seers and the memories of his dear Josephine, never far from his thoughts as long as they lived at The Elms, determined them to move. They combined house-hunting with Kipling's enthusiasm for the new and noisy motor-car. In 1899 he hired a single-cylinder, belt-driven Embryo together with an 'engineer' for 3½ guineas a week. The next year they bought a steam-driven Locomobile and went on long journeys through Sussex, often breaking down. On such a journey they found Bateman's in the village of Burwash near the Kent border. They fell in love with it on sight

A grey stone lichened house – AD 1634 over the door – beamed, panelled, with old oak staircase, and all untouched and unfaked. It is a good and peaceable place standing in terraced lawns nigh to a walled garden of old red brick, and two fat-headed oast houses with red brick stomachs, and an aged silver-grey dovecot on top. There is what they call a river at the bottom of the lawn.

Mrs Kipling left Bateman's to the National Trust and many of the rooms are as they were when her husband died. Hugh Walpole remembers Bateman's as 'an uncomfortable, hard-chaired home', and Elsie Kipling recalls

the stiff furniture and lack of comfort which my parents never seemed to notice – the whole effect was rather sparse and, in the winter, chilly in spite of the huge wood fire in the hall.

Kipling installed a turbine in the nearby mill to generate electricity for the house.

At Bateman's a new literary life began for Kipling. *Kim*, the last of his books about India, had just been published and he turned now to soak himself in England and its history and in particular, that of Sussex. Kipling was to do for Sussex what his friend Hardy had done for Dorset. *Puck of Pook's Hill* and *Rewards and Fairies* are a mingling of story and poetry that together strive to present Kipling's vision of England.

She is not any common Earth,
Water or wood or air,
But Merlin's Isle of Gramarye,
Where you and I will fare.

Rudyard Kipling   *Bateman's, Burwash*

But along with this magical, almost mystical, sense of England's destiny goes the quick and exact observation of the trained journalist that Kipling once was. His Sussex poems are full of beautiful miniatures – 'little, lost Down churches', 'our blunt, bow-headed, whale-backed Downs', 'close-bit thyme', 'the wooded, dim, blue goodness of the Weald'. The houses, the farms, and the landscape surrounding Burwash are all in these poems and stories; this part of Sussex is now Kipling country.

Free from the attentions of sightseers, there was none-the-less a steady stream of distinguished visitors to Bateman's – 150 in one year and most of them stayed overnight. Kipling knew a vast number of people all over the world but they were politicians, businessmen and professional soldiers rather than writers: Rider Haggard was one of the few writers with whom he corresponded regularly. Kipling admired the man of action rather than the thinker and his hard-line Conservative politics upset liberal-minded writers. He was derided then, as now, for being an imperialist and a missionary of Empire. He certainly believed that something terrible would befall Europe if the British Empire was not strong enough to prevent it.

Kipling died suddenly in London and his ashes were buried in Poet's Corner in Westminster Abbey. His pall-bearers included a Prime Minister, and Admiral and a General. The 'Recessional' was sung. He was a genuinely popular writer whose books were read by all sorts and conditions of men. During his lifetime his short stories sold 15 million copies in England and America. Since his death his reputation has declined along with the Empire he believed in but the core of his work will remain long after the arguments about politics are forgotten.

Bateman's is one of the most beautiful National Trust properties, ½ mile south of Burwash on the A265. Apart from the house interior, which is kept exactly as Kipling knew it, there are the gardens, a restored water mill which grinds corn, one of the oldest water-driven turbines in the world and Kipling's 1928 Rolls-Royce in the garage. There is also an excellent tea-room and shop.

Open: April to end October. Daily (closed Thursday and Friday) 11am – 6pm (last admission 5.30pm). Admission charge. Group reductions by pre-arrangement with the Administrator at special times (Telephone Burwash 882302).

Apart from going to Bateman's, which is a must, readers should also visit Rottingdean where they can not only admire the exterior of Kipling's house The Elms but also look at the permanent exhibition of Kipling memorabilia at a nearby Georgian house, The Grange, which also houses the public library. There are first editions of Kipling's books, twenty-six of his letters, portraits of him and some fine prints of the original illustrations to The Jungle Book.

17. W.B. Yeats *(1865–1939)*
Ezra Pound *(1885–1972)*

Coleman's Hatch &
Steyning.

In 1913, two poets, one Irish and the other American, moved into a small cottage at Coleman's Hatch on the northern edge of the Ashdown Forest. William Butler Yeats was forty-eight years of age and already famous for his poetry, his plays and his founding, with Lady Gregory, of the Abbey Theatre in Dublin.

Ezra Pound was twenty years younger then 'Uncle William' and although he was publishing a volume of poetry nearly every year, his work was read only by other writers. He had astounding energy: James Joyce described him as 'a large bundle of unpredictable electricity'. In addition to writing poetry, he edited literary journals and wrote an unceasing stream of articles – 117 in one year and 189 the next. Sir Herbert Read has also described him:

> Apart from his exotic appearance he rattled off his elliptic sentences with a harsh nasal twang, twitched incessantly, and prowled round the room like a caged panther. He was not made for compromise or for co-operation.

With yellow hair and a small red beard Pound was an eye-catching figure. His clothes were made at a good tailors in Holland Street: one overcoat had large square buttons of lapis lazuli. Sometimes he wore a floppy troubadour's hat with a single ear-ring. At one literary luncheon he declined the food, taking instead a rose from a bowl and eating it, petal by petal, with a knife and fork. He was witty, provocative, and charming.

Pound and Yeats shared Stone Cottage for three winters and springs from 1913 to 1916. Pound feared the worst, writing to his mother: 'My stay in Stone Cottage will not be in the least profitable. I detest the country. Yeats will amuse me part of the time and bore me to death with psychical research the rest. I regard the visit as a duty to posterity.' His fears were unfounded and a few weeks later he wrote to his mother again: 'I believe Sussex agrees with me quite nicely.' Pound acted as Yeats's secretary and in the evenings read Wordsworth to him. Yeats was having difficulty reading and writing as the sight of his left eye had almost gone and his other was very weak. It was while they were at the cottage that Yeats introduced Pound to the unpublished work of an unknown Irishman, James Joyce. From then on Pound worked tirelessly on Joyce's behalf, arranging for his work to be published and getting financial patronage for him. It is unlikely that either *Ulysses* or *Finnegan's Wake* would have been written without Pound's help. And there were many other writers he helped: D.H. Lawrence, T.S. Eliot, Robert Frost. He was midwife to twentieth-century literature, bringing new ideas and movements to birth. He encouraged new writers to keep writing and chivvied editors into publishing their work. His own work was constantly

W.B. Yeats and Ezra Pound   *Stone Cottage, Coleman's Hatch*

breaking new ground: in 1915 he published *Cathay*, a book of translations of Chinese poetry which caused Eliot to call him 'the inventor of Chinese poetry for our time'.

It was while they were at Stone Cottage that both poets married. One of Pound's Kensington friends was Mrs Olivia Shakespear. Her elderly husband was a wealthy solicitor and she was a novelist who liked to entertain fellow writers at her home. Pound wanted to marry her daughter, Dorothy. When Mr. Shakespear, with crushing realism, asked the poet how he could possibly manage to support a wife, Pound, undismayed, pulled a few bank notes from his pocket: 'I've got some money,' he said. Dorothy settled in contentedly at Stone Cottage with the two poets. In the first year of their marriage Pound earned exactly £42.

When Yeats and Olivia Shakespear were on a brief visit to Brighton, she introduced him to the Tuckers and their daughter Georgie; they had a house called The Prelude not far from Stone Cottage. Pound was best man at their wedding and part of the honeymoon was spent at Stone Cottage and part at Ashdown Forest Hotel in Forest Row. It was at the hotel that Yeats discovered that George – he refused to call her Georgie – practised automatic writing and had talents as a medium. This revived Yeats's earlier interest in the occult: he had once been a member of Mme. Blavatsky's Theosophical Society.

In 1920 the Pounds left England. Pound's politics took a dangerous turn when he made a hero of Mussolini and began dating his letters, in loyal Fascist style, from the Duce's 1922 March on Rome. In the 1930's Pound contributed several articles to the magazine of Sir Oswald Mosley's British fascist party and by the start of the war he was making propaganda broadcasts on Rome radio. The Americans refused to let him return to America and he remained in Italy, continuing to broadcast his rambling, abusive and often incoherent talks. It is difficult to see what propaganda value they

W.B. Yeats   *Chantry House, Steyning*

had for the Italian Government.

At the end of the war Pound gave himself up to the invading Allied forces. The Americans put him in a camp at Pisa where he was kept in a tiny wire cage in the open. After three weeks exposure to hot sun, dust and isolation, he collapsed and was moved to a small tent. During the rest of the time in the camp he wrote some of his finest poetry, the Pisan Cantos. In one passage he remembers the time that Yeats and he spent at Stone Cottage thirty years and a war ago:

> So that I recalled the noise in the chimney
> As it were, the wind in the chimney
> but was in reality Uncle William
> downstairs composing
> at Stone Cottage in Sussex by the waste moor
> (or whatever) and the holly bush . . .
> well those days are gone forever.

The holly bush is still in the back garden, and the waste moor of Ashdown Forest just over the garden hedge. Pound was taken back to the USA where he was charged with treason, declared insane and kept in a mental asylum for eleven years. He went back to Rapallo to die.

Yeats's connection with Sussex was renewed in 1935 when he became friendly with the poet Dorothy Wellesley. She invited Yeats to stay at her home, Penns in the Rocks, at Withyham, a few miles east of Coleman's Hatch: this was the first of many visits. Shortly afterwards, Edmund Dulac, who had designed the covers of several of Yeats's books, introduced him to Nora Heald and her sister Edith Shackleton Heald who lived in the lovely eighteenth-century Chantry House in Church Street, Steyning. Yeats stayed with the sisters on several occasions from 1937 onwards, writing some of his last poems there as well as his play *Purgatory*. Many years later when she was eighty, Edith Heald recalled those days: 'Most people think of Yeats as a great Irish patriot who could think only of Ireland, but this part of Sussex meant a great deal to him and he enjoyed car rides all round the district in the long summer months. He loved this house and garden and he loved the Sussex countryside.'

Stone Cottage can be found by starting from the Hatch pub in Coleman's Hatch village. Face the pub and take the road on its right. A short way along on the left is a narrow road through woods. Stone Cottage is on the left and the Prelude, now more appropriately called End House, is at the far end. The Chantry House is in Church Street, Steyning and has a commemorative plaque on the wall.

————————————

His father's import and export business seemed an unimaginative way of earning a living to young Tickner so he left London and took himself off to a cottage in the secluded village of Burpham on the River Arun.

Here he learned the difficult skills of journalism and bee-keeping, and succeeded in both. For many years he contributed articles on country life to magazines such as the *Pall Mall Gazette* while in his garden he watched the bees going in and out of his hives and carefully recorded their behaviour. He learned all he could from Sussex bee-keepers and at last he put his knowledge into two masterly books published in 1907 and 1908: *The Bee Master of Warrilow* and *The Lore of the Honey Bee*: a new edition of the former appeared in 1983. They were an immediate success. He had the gift of communicating solid and reliable information in an easy, readable style. His approach was scientific, yet he was able to give his readers a sense of the mysterious life of the hive. In the first book, he wrote: 'Warrilow is a precipitous village tucked away under the green brink of the Sussex downs.' It is of course Burpham and in later life Edwardes liked to be known as 'the bee-man of Burpham'.

The success of the bee books gave Edwardes' publisher the idea that a novel about bee-keeping might prove even more profitable. Edwardes was quick to agree, having always had a secret ambition to write romantic novels. *The Honey Star*, a story of primitive passions on a Sussex bee farm, appeared in 1913.

Several other romances followed, all in the same tradition of fruity village melodrama. The only one that became famous, *Tansy*, was about a beautiful village maiden who upsets farming conventions by working as a shepherdess. The book was read by Cecil Hepworth, a British film producer with a patriotic mission. Edwardes' book, set in the villages of Burpham, Amberley and North Stoke, was just what Hepworth wanted. With Alma Taylor in the star part he filmed it in Burpham in 1921 for a total cost of £8,000 and it was shown at 16,000 cinemas around the world. *Tansy* became a local legend and a thatched cottage, now demolished, at nearby Peppering, was pointed out to visitors as 'Tansy's cottage'. Edwardes was justly proud of the film's success and always kept in his study a signed photo of the charming Miss Taylor and himself in his black suit and clerical collar. The film is still hired at intervals by residents of Burpham and shown in the village.

Immediately after the Great War Edwardes went to theological college to train for the Anglican priesthood: he was now 53, a late age for a vocation. The War that destroyed the faith of some men seemed to strengthen Edwardes'. Perhaps in the ordered life of the bee, which he had spent so many years studying, he was able to see a divine pattern not discernible in human affairs. 'In spite of the War' he wrote 'the honey-bee remains the same mysterious, fascinating creature that she has ever been; and the men who live by the fruit of her toil share with her the like changeless

Tickner Edwardes

Red Cottage, Burpham

quality.' In 1920 he was ordained and served five years as a curate at Lyminster, north of Littlehampton. He was then Rector of Folkington, near Polegate, until he managed to get back to his beloved Burpham as vicar in 1927.

There are still some villagers who remember Tickner Edwardes as vicar. One of them said that every Christmas Eve he would visit the cottagers to give them half-a-crown, a present from the Duke of Norfolk, the local landowner. He was a friendly man but often walked about the village so deep in thought that he wouldn't notice if you said 'Good morning'. One villager remembered him for having started the village cricket team and another recalled what 'great walkers' the Edwardes family were: Mrs Edwardes could still walk to Petworth and back to give a talk at the Women's Institute – a round trip of about twenty miles – when she was eighty-five!

Apart from his bee books, the best of Edwardes is to be found in his books on country life. An early one, *Lift Luck on Southern Roads* (1910), is an account of the author's hitch-hike from Torquay, through Devon, Somerset, Wiltshire and

Hampshire to Sussex. He had lifts in farm wagons, tradesmen's carts, a parson's gig, a missionary's caravan, and once, rarest of all, in a motor car. Back on top of the Downs he slings his boots over his shoulder and walks bare-foot over the turf to Burpham. In later books he observes nature precisely and tenderly: after a lifetime's apprenticeship to the craft of writing the bee-master became a word-master. In the best tradition of nature writers he is always asking questions and only sometimes answering them. One day he peels a hummock of moss off a barn roof and discovers, with the aid of a magnifying glass, how it creates 'its own little fertile garden plot' on the bare slate. Then he is out on a 'warm, velvety dark' December night with a lantern watching the moths 'veering aimlessly to and fro'. A couple of days later he's chasing a flock of tweeting goldfinches over the fields until they disappear over ploughland. And writing in that first year of the Second World War, this gentle Sussex bee-keeper reflects,

> There are few things so pleasant to think of nowadays as the undoubted fact that the goldfinches are growing more plentiful in the English countryside every year.

Tickner Edwardes retired from the ministry in 1935 but lived on in Burpham until he died in 1944. He is buried in the church yard with this inscription on the headstone:

Tantorum amicus profecto amicos reperiet
A friend of many will certainly find friends.

Before reaching Burpham village the Burpham Country Hotel will be seen on the right hand side. This was originally the rectory and just beyond it, on the left, is Ilex Cottage, a small wooden thatched cottage that Edwardes had built ready for his retirement. Continue into Burpham, passing the Post Office and phone box on your left to the T junction. Turn right and immediately on your left behind a high yew hedge is Rycroft, a mid-Victorian red brick house which was Edwardes' home for many years. It was then known as Red Cottage.

———————————

It was a disaster for the Wells family when their father fell off the ladder and broke his hip; but for Herbert George, a clever and cocksure schoolboy, it was to pay unexpected dividends. The dingy little china shop in Bromley High Street had been losing money for years and now that father was laid up there would have to be another source of income. Unexpectedly a letter arrived inviting Mrs Wells to return to Uppark, the country mansion near Harting in Sussex where, many years earlier, she had worked as a maid and met and married Mr Wells the gardener; now she was to return as housekeeper.

Two of her three sons were off her hands, apprenticed to the drapery trade and H.G. was doomed to follow them. Having left school at fourteen he was sent on trial to a draper's in Windsor where he worked from 7.30 in the morning to 8.30 at night for sixpence a week pocket money and board and lodging. He made his loathing so obvious by shirking his work that his mother was soon asked to remove him. Hearing that a relative of hers was starting a school in Wookey, Somerset, she fixed H.G. up with a post as pupil-teacher. It lasted only three months; Uncle William was a decidedly bogus character and the local education board soon discovered that his teaching qualifications were forged. Leaving Wookey, the young Wells joined his mother at Uppark. It was a splendid seventeenth-century stately home, built on the side of Harting Hill, with deer feeding under the shadow of great beech trees and the coast of Sussex and Hampshire spread out beneath it. Here, as the housekeeper's son, Wells was given the liberty of borrowing books from the great library. The house belonged to the Fetherstonhaugh family and Sir Harry, one of the Prince Regent's cronies, had been a free-thinker and had added many books by Voltaire, Tom Paine and other 'advanced' thinkers. Wells dipped into them all, finding there 'the amazing and heartening suggestion that the whole fabric of law, custom and worship, which seemed so invincibly established, might be cast into the melting pot and made anew'. They confirmed all his own rebellious thoughts and feelings, especially his contempt for religion.

Mrs Wells was not content for her son to waste his time reading books at Uppark. She arranged for him to work at a chemist's shop in Midhurst in the hope that he might become a pharmacist. Wells liked Midhurst; it was only 'three hours sturdy walking' from Uppark and it had family associations as Mrs Wells's father had once kept an inn there. Wells liked the chemist's shop with its 'drawers full of squills and senna pods, flowers of sulpher, charcoal and suchlike curious things'. And he liked Mr Cowap the chemist who appears, many years later, as Uncle Ponderevo in the novel *Tono-Bungay*. As Wells was ignorant of Latin and was unable to read prescriptions, he was given lessons by the Head of Midhurst Grammar School. But the new career soon foundered when it was decided that the fees for qualifying as a

H.G. Wells   *Uppark, South Harting*

chemist were far beyond Mrs Wells's means. Until she could arrange a new start for Wells she paid for him to board at the Grammar School. Wells is proud to record that the Head was astonished at his quickness of mind 'accustomed as he was to working against the resistances of Sussex tradesmen's and farmer's sons and the like'.

Mrs Wells left him there for two months and then sent him to Southsea to try the drapery trade again: it seemed to her the only secure and respectable employment for people in their station of life. But her son had no intention of being buried alive: he stuck it dutifully for two years and then, threatening suicide, refused to stay there any longer. On an impulse he wrote to the Head of Midhurst Grammar School asking for a post as an under-master and, at the age of seventeen, was appointed. He shared rooms with another teacher above a sweet shop next to the Angel Hotel in North Street. At last he had work that matched his intellectual ambitions. Encouraged by the Head, he crammed for exams in the sciences. When the exam results were known he had enough firsts to qualify as an external student at the School of Science in South

Kensington under the great Professor Thomas Huxley. And he was awarded a grant of one guinea a week.

He spent more time debating religion and socialism than studying and as a consequence he failed his degree. It was a blow to his self-esteem. With his scientific career in ruins, he took a teaching post in Wales. During a football match a kick in the back ruptured a kidney and he spent three months convalescing at Uppark. When he recovered he returned to London and never lived in Sussex again. But it was not forgotten: 'I know of no country to compare with West Sussex except the Cotswolds,' he wrote, and its villages and towns are recreated in his novels. In *Tono-Bungay* Midhurst appears as Wimblehurst – 'an exceptionally quiet and grey Sussex town, rare among south of England towns in being largely built of stone. I found something very agreeable and picturesque in its clean, cobbled streets, its odd turnings and abrupt corners, and in the pleasant park that crowds up on one side of the town.' The chemist's shop is in the same book and also Uppark though it is transported to Kent and renamed Bladesover. Wells's experience as a teacher went into *Love and Mr Lewisham* and one of his earliest novels, *The Wheels of Chance*, published in 1896, was set in Sussex. Wells was a keen cyclist and prepared for writing the book by taking to the road with a notebook in his hip-pocket. The book's hero, Mr Hoopdriver, cycles in pursuit of the villain through a long chain of Sussex villages. Wells boasted that 'wherever Hoopdriver rode, I rode'. The chase began in the little sweet-shop in Midhurst, where Wells had once lodged.

The Midhurst Grammar School is still where it was in North Street and the tile-hung Tuck Shop where Wells lodged is still next to the Angel Hotel, also in North Street. At the top of Church Hill is the chemist's shop.

Uppark, built about 1690, is set high on the downs 5 miles south-east of Petersfield on the B2146, 1½ miles south of South Harting. In this National Trust property the Victorian kitchen and the housekeeper's room where Wells's mother presided can be seen, as well as other rooms, with original furnishings and fabrics. The garden, landscaped by Repton, is a superb setting for the tea-room (2.30–5.30 on open days).

Open: April to end of September. Wednesdays, Thursdays, Sundays and Bank Holiday Mondays only. 2pm–6pm (last admission 5.30pm). Admission charge. (Reductions for pre-booked parties: Telephone the Administrator on Harting 317 or 458).

20. John Galsworthy *(1867–1933)* Bury

For many years John Galsworthy and his wife, Ada, had been in the habit of staying in hotels at Littlehampton to escape the London fogs. John liked their farmhouse in Devon but Ada preferred the sea.

But it was John who impulsively brought the splendid 15-bedroomed Bury House at Bury, 4 miles north of Arundel. In 1926 the stone Tudor-style mansion in the quiet village by the River Arun cost £9,000. It was much too big for the two of them so they installed a nephew and his wife as caretakers and culled the village for servants and the five gardeners needed to keep the extensive grounds in order.

At 59, Galsworthy was at the height of his career as a successful writer. He had published more than a dozen novels and the *Forsyte Saga* had brought him unanimous acclaim. He had the distinction of having refused a knighthood proffered by Lloyd George. At Bury House he continued to write compulsively. *Swan Song*, in which old Soames Forsyte dies, was followed by *On Forsyte Change*, the last of the Forsyte series. As the curtain fell on one family saga it rose on another – the Cherrells. He wrote three books about this family finishing the last – *Over The River* – in the summer of 1932. In January of the following year he was dead.

As well as writing he persisted with his lifelong habit of physical exercise, horse riding on the downs, tennis, croquet on the lawn and cricket matches with the village team. On top of all this, Ada, an indefatigable hostess, was arranging an unending stream of distinguished visitors for summer weekends. J.M. Barrie, Hugh Walpole, Philip Guedalla and John Drinkwater were frequent visitors and Arnold Bennett, embarrassingly vulgar, would arrive in his Rolls Royce and boast about his yacht.

Galsworthy was extremely wealthy and extremely successful, yet he was deeply dissatisfied both with himself and with his work. When, shortly before he died, he was awarded the Nobel Prize for Literature, he wrote that he was afraid

> of that moment when I shall have said all I have to say, and must wait till life slips behind me, says, 'Time, sir,' and I answer, 'You have been long in coming. Here is my pen – the ink in it is dry. Take it and give it to some other who will serve you better.'

Perhaps he felt that his success was, in a way, a kind of defeat, a betrayal of his own high principles. It was he, after all, who, in *The Forsyte Saga* had mercilessly satirised the 'man of property'. Had Galsworthy now become the sort of man whose values he had for so long despised? Had he, in short, become a Forsyte?

Galsworthy protested against what he regarded as the hypocrisy, greed and false values of late Victorian England. He saw himself as the conscience of society, and the voice of moral rectitude, of kindness and compassion. Philip Gibbs, the writer, has left this recollection of Galsworthy:

Some people were put off by his style and manner. They thought him a snob, whereas he loved the common man – farmers and sheep-shearers and all rustic folk. But he had never known poverty. His clothes were cut by the best tailor; he bought his boots at Lobb's; he was in every sense of the word that somewhat old-fashioned type in this careless age, 'an English gentleman'. Yet when I was an impecunious journalist, shabbily dressed, he was charming to me and was not above drinking a cup of weak coffee with me in an ABC round the corner in Fleet Street.

He was, undoubtedly, a kind man to any who went to him for help and during his years at Bury the social reformer in him survived as a philanthropist: every Friday a servant would go round the village with a basketful of white envelopes containing five or ten shilling 'pensions' that he allotted to those in need. That servant still lives in Bury, and the cottages that he built for those who worked at Bury House can still be seen in the village. Yet the very novels he wrote castigating society for its 'money-values' made him one of the richest living writers. He was not the first or the last

John Galsworthy

Bury House, Bury

'angry young man' to live long enough to become a respected figure of the Establishment.

Shortly before Galsworthy died he was taken to his London house where half-a-dozen specialists could attend him: their efforts were to no avail. He faced death with difficulty having no religious faith and having lost faith in himself. Even his moral fortitude, his stiff upper lip, was trembling. His nephew took his ashes from Woking Crematorium and scattered them in the downs above Bury, the downs where every morning he had loved to ride.

During the Second World War, Galsworthy's house became first an officers' mess for the gun battery up on Bury Hill and later was used to house evacuees from London. After the War it was bought by West Sussex County Council and is now an elderly people's home. At the head of the oak staircase is a fine portrait of Galsworthy in oils. The Matron, Sheila Wyatt, welcomes visitors. Please telephone Bury (079881) 756.

The popularity of Tressell's novel *The Ragged Trousered Philanthropists* has made him into a working-class folk hero. But Tressell himself was not in the least a working-class sterotype: he read Plato, Aristotle and Shakespeare, took his daughter to Gilbert and Sullivan operas and every weekend he bought himself a button-hole at a local florist's.

His origins are uncertain but it seems that he was born in Dublin and his father was a British Army officer. Disagreements with the family caused him to cut short his education and emigrate to South Africa in the early 1890s. There he learned the trade of house painter and sign-writer. He also taught himself Dutch and acquired a smattering of German and Spanish. There was a brief marriage, ended either by separation or the death of his wife, no one knows which, leaving Tressell with a daughter, Kathleen.

On the eve of the Boer War Tressell was joined in South Africa by a widowed sister and her son and it was decided that the two fragmented families should sail for England and set up home together. Tressell paid all the fares and they arrived in Hastings in 1902 taking the top floor flat at 1 Plynlimmon Road, overlooking the gas works and the town. Shortly afterwards they moved into another top floor flat, at 115 Milward Road where they stayed for three years. Disagreements between brother and sister had now reached the point where it was clearly better to separate: she was particularly anxious to protect her son from Tressell's forthrightly expressed views on politics and religion. Tressell and Kathleen moved to rooms at 241 London Road, over a cycle shop, where they remained for the rest of his life in Hastings.

Tressell was now working for local firms as a decorator and sign-writer. As a skilled artisan he was paid sevenpence an hour, a rate which put him a cut above the ordinary working man. As if to mark this difference Tressell always wore a trilby hat at work, never the cloth cap which was then the badge of the worker. Life in the building trade then was unimaginably hard compared with today: the worker had to be on the job at six a.m. which often entailed a journey on foot of an hour or more. Tressell was a consumptive and his health must have been worsened by wet journeys and working all day in damp clothes. Arriving a few minutes late could mean the sack at a time when jobs were few and far between. The day ended at 5.30 and there were no holidays. In Hastings, in Tressell's day, there were 390 people in the workhouse and 147 registered vagrants. Many hundreds were on the 'charity' and there were daily queues at soup kitchens.

Tressell's militant socialism and atheism found an outlet at work where he was always trying to convince the 'cloth caps' of the injustice of 'the system' that exploited them and explain how they could put it right. He was as often infuriated by their stupidity and ingrained conservatism as they were baffled by his long words and his enthusiasm for 'the cause'. He joined the Hastings branch of the Social Democratic Federation which met in a room at the Cricketers' Pub. The SDF – ridiculed as the Silly Damned Fools – was too dogmatically Marxist ever to succeed with the English worker and it was soon eclipsed by the newly formed Labour Party. The SDF held open air meetings under a red flag in the Fishmarket. Tressell's voice was always too weak for public speaking but he wrote leaflets, did posters and banners and lent his own books out at a penny a time to educate the workers. It was in the room above the cycle shop that Tressell noted down, after each day's work, the banter and back-chat of his work mates. He recorded the ups and downs of their lives, the cat and mouse games they played with the foremen, their courage in the face of hardship and misery. He also exposed the petty meannesses of the employers, skimping and saving to make a bit of extra money on every job: two coats of paint instead of the estimated three, covering up cracks and dirt with a coat of whitewash, promising the customer the best materials but supplying the cheapest. To Tressell, disciple of William Morris, these money-mad employers were the whited sepulchres of the building trade. He respected good workmanship and to him the shoddy and the sub-standard were a kind of blasphemy. It is a vivid picture of the Hastings of his day spoiled only by his incurable habit of lecturing his workmates, and the reader.

The book took him five years to complete, copying 250,000 words onto nearly 1,700 quarto sheets. He then had a tin box specially made so that the manuscript could be posted to publishers. It was sent to three without success. It seems that the failure of his book and his worsening health decided Tressell on emigrating to Canada. Once on his feet he would send for Kathleen who was eighteen and had just finished at High School. In the summer of 1910 he left Hastings for Liverpool but there he was taken ill and the following February died. He was buried in an unmarked pauper's grave.

Shortly afterwards Kathleen sold the manuscript of the book to a publisher for £25 and it was published in a severely abridged form in 1914: it sold about two thousand copies. A cheaper edition appeared in 1918 and the General Strike of 1926 helped to boost its sales. Trade unions helped to promote it and it was even used as a textbook at the London School of Economics. In 1955, Lawrence & Wishart, publishers to the Communist Party of Great Britain, put out the first unabridged edition. In 1967 it was dramatised and was shown on TV. In the rush to exploit the book's political message, Tressell's own purpose in writing the book seems forgotten: in the preface he writes –

> My object was to write a readable story full of human interest and based on the happenings of everyday life, the subject of socialism being treated incidentally.

115 Milward Road, at the back of Hastings Castle, has a plaque on the front wall. Other memorials in Hastings are a seat on the front with a dedicatory plate and a road, Robert Tressell Close.

Belloc loved Sussex as few other writers have loved her: he lived there for most of his eighty-three years, he tramped the length and breadth of the county, slept under her hedgerows, drank in her inns, sailed her coast and her rivers and wrote several incomparable books about her.

Belloc was a Catholic but Sussex was a pagan religion to him in which the old gods were brought back to life. The valley of the western Rother, the scene of his boyhood, was 'like a shrine in England' and the Rother itself 'the sacred and fruitful river'. A list of place names became a prayer

> The river Arun, a valley of sacred water; the Amberley Wild brook, which is lonely with reeds at evening; and Burton Great house, where I had spent nights in November; and Lavington also and Hidden Byworth; and Fittleworth next on, and Egdean Side, all heath and air; and the lake and the pine trees at the mill; and Petworth, little town. All the land which is knit in with our flesh.

Belloc was born in France of a French father and an English mother. His father died when he was very young and his mother brought Hilaire to England, living first in London, and then, when he was eight years old, in Slindon, in what is now known as the Dower House. (Belloc's mother later moved to Gaston Cottage where she lived until she died at the age of 95.) He was a physically restless boy, and it was then that he formed the habit of long walks that would last a lifetime. Before he was fourteen he had walked from Petersfield to Beachy Head, a four or five days' tramp, sleeping rough. After several unsuccessful attempts to earn a living, he fell in love with a young American girl he met by chance in London. She was intent on trying her vocation in a religious order and refused to marry him. Belloc was determined that she should. When she returned to America he followed her, penniless, from New York to California, where she lived. Rejected again, he returned to England. Six years later, they were married.

The responsibilities of a family compelled Belloc to set about earning his living by writing. He had an extraordinary gift for rapid composition: to write his biography of King James II, he stayed in a small hotel on the edge of the Sahara Desert, wrote for ten hours a day and finished the 75,000 word book in eight days. In forty-six years Belloc wrote over 150 works. This would be a remarkable achievement for a sedentary author like Belloc's friend G.K. Chesterton, but Belloc was a man of action as well as a writer and was always on the move. He was also a man who loved the company of friends, talking and singing and drinking far into the night. No one has ever explained how Belloc found time to write.

By 1905 Belloc had five children, and living in Cheyne Walk at Chelsea was proving too expensive for him. He took a lease of Courthill Farm, a Georgian house on the north-western outskirts of Slindon, enabling him to return to the scenes of his youth. But the move to Slindon was not a success and eighteen months later they moved to the tiny village of Shipley, on the other side of the Arun.

Belloc bought King's Land, five acres and a working windmill for £1,000 and it became his home for the rest of his life. The miller brought their belongings over from Slindon in two farm carts. The long brick house, built by monks as a tithe barn, had been the village shop back in the eighteenth century: the shop became the living-room, the store rooms became the nursery and the old bacon room the schoolroom. Belloc had the dining-room, with its stone-flagged floor and open fire, panelled in oak. Down its length ran the oak refectory table which had once belonged to an Oxford college and which the Bellocs had bought for £10 in a second-hand shop. Upstairs were several bedrooms and a room that they made into a family chapel where a priest from the monastery at Storrington would sometimes say Mass. The house was lit by candles and oil lamps for as long as Belloc lived there. He refused to

Hilaire Belloc

Shipley Mill

77

Hilaire Belloc   Courthill Farmhouse, Slindon

have a telephone installed at King's Land although, visiting friends' houses, he always
made a bee-line for the phone, meticulously reckoning and paying the cost of
his call.

One thing Belloc never lacked was friends: they were there when his wife died in
1914 when Belloc was only thirty-four, when his eldest son was killed in the First
World War and when another son died in the Second World War. After his wife's
death he always wore black. He always had friends to crew his sailing boat, the Nona.
Belloc had been taught sailing when a boy by a Slindon man in Chichester harbour
and knew the South Coast and the Sussex waterways well. The Nona was moored at
Littlehampton and sometimes he would sail it up the Arun as far as Stopham. After
sailing round the coast of England he wrote *The Cruise of the Nona* which tells us more

about Belloc than any other of his books. And lastly, there were friends for drinking in Sussex inns and singing the boisterous drinking songs that Belloc loved.

> From Crowboro' Top to Ditchling Down,
> From Hurstpierpoint to Arundel town,
> The girls are plump and the ale is brown
> Which nobody can deny, deny.

The names of the inns of Sussex are scattered through Belloc's books like holy places for the pilgrims of an irreligious age: there they can receive the blessings of blazing fire and frothing ale. The George at Robertsbridge, the Bridge Inn at Amberley, the White Hart at Storrington, the Swan at Petworth, the White Horse at Steyning, the Fountain at Ashurst. From Shipley, Belloc used to ride his Sunbeam bicycle to the Spread Eagle at Midhurst. In later years he would drive his Ford Model T Tourer to West Grinstead for Mass and a drink at the Tabby Cat Inn. He had a weekly barrel of ale from the brewery at Steyning and imported wine from France by the barrel, bottling it himself.

Belloc in his prime was a massive bulk of a man with an enormous and resolute jaw. His friend Lady Diana Cooper had a small-holding at Bognor during the last War and recalls a visit by Belloc, then in his seventies: 'He was frightfully decrepit, poor old saint, moved as slowly as a tortoise and was covered with gravy, ash and candlegrease. He could not move or get up without some support, and so always carried a very frayed umbrella.' Belloc, pierced by the thought of his own mortality, wrote:

> He does not die that can bequeath
> Some influence to the land he knows,
> Or dares, persistent, interwreath
> Love permanent with the wild hedgerows;
> He does not die, but still remains
> Substantiate with his darling plains.

Belloc appealed to the spirits of weald and down to perpetuate his name; he did not appeal in vain.

Shipley Mill, built in 1879, is the biggest smock mill in Sussex. Repairs were financed by Belloc's friends as a memorial. It is open to the public on the first weekend of every month May to October inclusive, 2.30–5.30pm. There is a small Belloc museum containing his walking-stick and pipe and other belongings. Belloc's house at Shipley, which is not open to the public, is still in the family, owned by his grandson. Some of the rooms are just as they were when Belloc died: the clock from his yacht Nona still ticks in the kitchen and memorial cards to his two sons killed in the wars, pinned by Belloc to the walls of the tiny chapel, are still there. In his wife's bedroom, locked by him on the day she died and never opened again, are her dresses and coats and Edwardian hats with ostrich feathers. Belloc's grave is at the Catholic Church at West Grinstead.

Famous at 24 and dead at 28, he had the shortest life of any writer in this book; 'a brutal, needless extinction' as Henry James, his fellow American said. Crane arrived in England in 1897 after covering the war between Greece and Turkey as a newspaperman. He brought with him Cora, formerly mistress of a Jacksonville brothel, who passed as his wife; Mrs Ruedy, a friend of Cora's; Ptolemy, a Greek butler, and Valestino, a puppy he had rescued from the battlefield. They settled into Ravensbrook House at Oxted in Surrey. Valestino died soon afterwards and was buried amongst the rhododendrons.

Crane's was a difficult, angular personality, ironic in outlook, abrupt in speech and often arrogant. 'I could never do what I didn't feel like doing – not even writing.' For some years he had hung about the Bowery in New York amongst the human derelicts and wrote a novel. *Maggie: a girl of the streets.* It was too harshly realistic to interest publishers so he had it printed at his own expense. But it didn't sell and when it was cold he lit the fire with unsold copies. These were years of poverty relieved by occasional work as a journalist.

The breakthrough came with his story of the American Civil War, *The Red Badge of Courage.* When it was first published the critics in America took little notice, but in England Crane was hailed as a genius. The Americans soon recognized their mistake and sales soared to 13 editions in ten months. Ambrise Bierce said it was written with blood not ink yet at the time Crane had never had a whiff of battle smoke. But he was a child when the Civil War was still fresh in men's minds and he refought the battles of Gettysburg and Chancellorsville with buttons on the kitchen floor. As a youth he listened for hours to the talk of war veterans and to his brother William who had studied the strategy of the War.

He arrived in England to find everyone reading his book and wanting to talk to him. He had money for the first time in his life and a home where he could entertain friends. Cora and Stephen were soon overwhelmed with visitors. Friends, fellow writers, and even people they had never heard of would turn up uninvited and stay for days. They entertained lavishly and thought nothing of spending £3 or £4 on flowers for the dinner table. Crane knew it could not go on forever; he was spending not earning. But how could he write in a houseful of people? Escaping for a few days to a London hotel to finish a short story was not the answer. He sent it to his agent, pleading – 'For heaven's sake raise me all the money you can and cable it.' The following year he was commissioned to report the war that had just broken out in Cuba between Spain and America. He was ill with consumption and his health could only be worsened by the physical hardships of the campaign. But he felt compelled to test himself against the reality of battle. Eyewitnesses testify to his suicidal indifference to bullets. He never had any interest in longevity and once said that 35 years would be his limit.

In England, Cora, desperately short of money, was summonsed for debt and the house was seized by the bailiffs. Crane came back and a friend rescued them by the loan, rent free, of Brede Place, near Rye in Sussex. Nothing could have been worse for Crane's health than a cold, damp, medieval manor house in a river valley. It was every American's idea of an English lord's country seat: it had a portcullis, an owl's nest, an ancient butler, a ghost and primitive plumbing. The Cranes were wildly incongruous tenants, with Cora in smock and sandals cooking doughnuts and Stephen playing poker in the great hall with his cronies. They had half-a-dozen dogs and two horses, Hengist and Horsa, which Crane rode like a cowboy. Sometimes he would practise with his revolver on the lawn. He would write upstairs in the long study. *Harper's Magazine* was using a new story by him every month and a collection of stories, *The Open Boat* had just come out; another, *Wounds in the Rain* was to follow. He was eating less and smoking less. He knew he was dying but refused to see doctors. His friends worried but he wrote to them privately telling them not to mention his health in front of Cora; 'I'm just a dry twig on the edge of a bonfire' he said.

Crane's compatriot, Henry James, lived at Rye and two or three times a week he would cycle over. Henry was often embarrassed by the Cranes who, in his view, had no sense of the proprieties of English life, but he was deeply fond of young Crane, exactly half his age; they shared the same intense fidelity to writing. Conrad was another novelist friend. Crane loved dogs and horses and children: adults he treated more warily. H.G. Wells lived at nearly Sandgate in Kent and described Crane as

> a lean, blond, slow-speaking, perceptive, fragile, tuberculous being, too adventurous to be temperate with anything and impracticable to an extreme degree. How he managed ever to get to the seats of war to which he was sent I cannot imagine.

Wells was at the Christmas party at Brede Place in 1899. There were thirty or forty guests who brought their own blankets and put up in varying degrees of discomfort. The revelling went on into the early hours and the medieval sanitation of Brede Place was revealed in the morning when Wells saw from the window 'the wintry countryside dotted with wandering, melancholy, preoccupied men guests'. At the end of the party they drank a toast to the twentieth century, Crane suddenly collapsed with a haemorrhage and Wells cycled off into the drizzling dawn for a doctor.

When Henry James, who was not at the party, heard the bad news he rushed up to London for an American doctor who had arrived from New York. With his unfailing kindness he cabled a shop in America to send a hamper of New England delicacies so that Crane could taste again 'the fierce joys' of pumpkin pie, apple butter, clams and soft shell crabs. In a last effort to save Crane, Cora took him to Dover and thence to the Black Forest in Germany. On June 5th, Henry James wrote to Cora enclosing a cheque for £50: 'dedicate it to whatever service may best render my stricken young friend. It meagrely represents my tender benediction to him.' Crane died as James was writing the letter. The body was brought back to London, taken to New Jersey and buried in the Crane family grave in Evergreen Cemetery. The £50 helped to pay the funeral expenses.

The 15th century Brede Place, near the village of Brede on the A28, was once described by Sir Edwin Lutyens as 'the most interesting inhabited house in England'. The house has several resident ghosts and when Canadian soldiers were stationed there during the last war they did night sentry duties in pairs. In the 1970s it was badly damaged by fire and is now being restored. Twenty years ago the house was open to the public one day a week but the present owners do not welcome visitors.

---

24. John Cowper Powys *(1872–1963)*   Southwick, Offham & Burpham

John Cowper Powys first came to Sussex in 1893. He had just graduated from Cambridge and had taken a post lecturing in literature at two girls' schools at Brighton. As he travelled down by train from London to Lewes, he sketched the face of Sussex:

> Those huge Sussex barns whose vast sloping roofs were encrusted with orange-coloured lichen . . . those mellow Sussex cottages whose old dark woodwork was so cunningly used in with brickwork and flintwork, those Sussex bricks themselves that were so much brighter and gayer than the red bricks of my native Midlands . . . those enormous Sussex wagons, painted blue and scarlet . . . the trim, neat picturesque Sussex villages . . . the great downs themselves, like huge waves solidified into chalk and turf.

He earned £5 a week lecturing and his father, who was vicar of Montacute in Somerset, made him an allowance of £60 a year. For £1 a week he rented a couple of rooms above Pollard's grocers shop in Albion Street, Southwick. He had a back bedroom and a bow-windowed room overlooking the harbour. In later life he recalled that the room smelt of sardines. It was here that he gave his first public lecture: it was on English literature at Hove Town Hall and the audience consisted of three women and a child.

After a few years at Southwick, Powys moved to Court House, an isolated farmhouse at Offham tucked under the north slope of the Downs. He qualified as a University Extension lecturer and began travelling by train all over England lecturing to mainly working-class audiences on literature and philosophy. He once described himself as an 'actor-priest' and lecturing was to become for him as necessary an activity as writing. He used to walk the four miles to Lewes to catch the train carrying his gown and his heavy books in what he called his 'ferret-bag'. On the long train journeys he read the novels of Dickens and Hardy and ate 'enormous quantities of raw sweet chocolate', a habit forced on him partly by the gastric ulcers that plagued him all his life.

From Court House Powys made frequent excursions to Eastbourne and Brighton to buy second-hand books. In Eastbourne he found one that specialised in erotica and at Brighton he adventured with street girls. 'I gave myself up' he writes 'to neurotic aberrations which must constantly have wavered and toppled on the verge of madness.' In fact he did nothing much worse than lie on Brighton beach ogling girls' ankles. Later in life he recalled Brighton front with its 'smells of seaweed and fish and tar and sweat and sandwiches and rope and paint and cheap perfumes and foam-drenched petticoats and bilge-water and beer'. Another of his pleasures was Warningore Wood near Offham:

> a wonderful wood of oaks and hazels and elms and beeches. To this wood I would almost

daily repair, and penetrating into the centre of it walk up and down a narrow mossy path, sprinkled in autumn by crimson toadstools and in spring by white violets . . . sufficient reward for having been born upon this cruelly-blasted planet!

While at Court House, Powys married Margaret Lyon, sister of a friend from his university days. Powys arranged for the words 'With my body I thee worship' to be left out of the marriage service: he dreaded intercourse with a virgin and it was months before the marriage was consummated. She was expecting her first child when they moved, in 1902, westwards across the Adur River to Burpham on the banks of the Arun where Powys paid £500 for Warre House, also known as Bankside. He was jealous of his privacy and had his first-floor study shut off from the rest of the house by double-doors. He was displeased to find that the village children played on top of the high embankment, an old Saxon earthwork, that bounded one side of the garden and he put a huge board labelled 'Trespassers Will Be Prosecuted' on the embankment. The villagers promptly threw it into the ditch and a second board was treated in the same summary fashion.

John Cowper Powys   *Warre House, Burpham*

84

The road that leads to Burpham village is a dead-end so that even today Burpham preserves a seclusion that most other villages have lost. At the turn of the century it must have been rarely visited by strangers. In his autobiography, Powys says that

> the great event of the year was the sheepwashing which took place in a narrow estuary of the river. Early in the morning a vast continuous stream of woolly sheep would pour down the lane past our house, filling the whole space between the walls, and making a peculiar sound unlike anything else.

In the winter of 1904–5, Powys was invited to lecture in America. Lecturing paid better there than in England and his tour was very successful. From now on most winters were spent there. Since the birth of their son, Margaret had engaged two maids, an unnecessary extravagance in the opinion of some of their friends. As their son grew up there was the further expense of his education and Powys was often forced to borrow money from his brothers. In 1907 he had to abandon lecturing when he collapsed with violent stomach pains. An ulcer was removed in the London Hospital and he convalesced at Bognor.

Their marriage was doomed from the beginning: Margaret was a thoroughly conventional woman who was intolerant of his oddities and he defiantly resisted her attempts to make him respectable. She was a devoutly religious woman attending the village church where the curate was a close friend of hers. She must often have been shocked by her husband's seemingly blasphemous views.

Powys' first novel, *Wood and Stone* was published in America in 1915 and *Rodmoor* was published the following year. In 1919 he began a novel called *After My Fashion* with Sussex for its setting. In April 1920 he returned from America and spent three months writing at Burpham. In this novel, as in *Rodmoor*, he dramatised his marriage failure as a struggle between the demands of domesticity and genius. He continued to support his wife and son and to pay occasional visits to them whenever he was in England but as the American climate suited his health he tended to spend more time in that country. In 1928 his financial burdens were eased and his connection with Burpham and Sussex ended when his wife let the house to a tenant and went to live at Folkestone with their son.

The grocer's shop in Southwick has been demolished. Court House, on the B2116 at Offham, near Lewes, bears little resemblance now to what it was when Powys lived there.

Warre House, Burpham has been renamed Frith House. It stands behind high flint walls near the George and Dragon Inn.

25. A.E. Coppard   *(1878–1957)*   Brighton

Alfred Edgar Coppard was born in Folkestone but both his parents were Brighton bred. When his father lost his tailoring job he walked the hundred miles back to Brighton and found himself another at the cavalry barracks at Preston, stitching gold braid onto officers' tunics. His wife joined him later with Alfie and two daughters; later, there would be a third. After lodging with another tailor, they moved to a tiny terraced cottage in Melbourne Street. This was the first of a succession of lodgings, all in the north-eastern quarter of Brighton, where the arches of the newly-built viaduct carried the railway over the Lewes Road to Kemp Town. It was not the most fashionable part of the town but it was a paradise compared with the slums of Sussex Street and Carlton Hill down in the middle of the town. And the cottage was only five shillings a week from a man who made tombstones.

For a short time Alfie spent his school days as a paraffin vendor's boy, shouting 'Oil, Oil!' at every street corner. Then his father, who was only twenty-nine years old, died of consumption: Brighton at that time had a worse record for deaths from this disease than Liverpool. Unable to cope with all her children, his mother sent Alfie to London's East End to lodge with Uncle Harry and to learn tailoring at Mr Abraham's, where women made trousers for one and ninepence a pair: there is a portrait of Mr Abrahams in Coppard's story *The Presser*. It was the Whitechapel of Jack the Ripper's activities and the dirt and noise of city life were alien to Alfie. Looking back on it all at the end of his life, Coppard wrote:

> It was there that I lost childhood, innocence, schooling, and became acquainted with grief, starvation, poor clothes and slums.

Returning to Brighton for a holiday he tearfully persuaded his mother to let him stay.

Another mouth to fill and an increase of sixpence in the rent forced her to pack their belongings on a handcart and move to a couple of rooms in Hollingdean Road. She was working at a laundry at the corner of the Steine, twenty-seven pence for a twelve-hour day. The Parish Relief gave her 7/6d a week and some loaves and flour. Later moves took them to two rooms in Newmarket Road and finally to three rooms on the upper floor of a house in Gladstone Place.

The truth of Disraeli's contention that England was two nations, the Rich and the Poor, the Privileged and the People, was plainly evident in Brighton at the end of the Victorian age. A mile from the cottages where the Coppards lived was the heart of fashionable society. One of Alfie's first jobs, office boy at Jenner and Dells, the estate agents, took him every day down Preston Street towards the sea front:

> In that paradise of brightness the classic Brighton front with its grand hotels and shops, its bath-chairs perambulating fat old gentlemen, growlers waiting amiably for a fare, and

goat-chaises with aristocratic children attached to spades and shrimping nets, radiated in a vast sparkle of never-ending sunlight from Hove to the Old Chain Pier.

Many other jobs followed: at nineteen he was a despatch clerk at Jordan's, the carriers, who had a large and gloomy warehouse, close by Brighton railway station, stacked with cases of Sunlight Soap and sacks of Hovis flour. These and other goods were sent out to the shops in Brighton by horse-van. After two or three years there, he got a better job as a cashier at a new engineering works opposite the Barracks on the Lewes Road. Although a dunce at arithmetic when he was at school, he now found that he could manipulate figures easily. When he was given an office of his own and a rise in wages, he was able to persuade his mother to give up her work at the laundry.

Coppard was entirely self-educated. What spare money he had he spent on second-hand books and much of his spare time he spent in Brighton Public Library reading poetry and Elizabethan plays. He had come under the spell of poetry at the age of sixteen when, sheltering under the awning of a second-hand book shop, he read Keats' 'La Belle Dame Sans Merci'. When Frank Benson's touring company brought Shakespeare to the Theatre Royal, Coppard was up in the sixpenny gallery. He entered a literary competition run by the *West Sussex Gazette* and won 2nd place for a descriptive piece on the Ouse Valley: he chose Chaucer's poems for his prize. But at this time he had no ambition to be a writer.

Coppard was always a boy with a great fund of animal energy; he bowled, batted, boxed, swam, ran, played football at outside-right and also billiards and cards. Athletics he took very seriously. He entered for cross-country races before realising that he was a born sprinter. He practised running on Brighton's Race Course and became a first-class professional. He won many silver medals for sprint races but always gave them away to admirers: he wanted money prizes so that he could buy more books.

When Coppard was twenty-seven he married a stenographer who worked in his office. For about a year they lived at Burdock Farm, Burgess Hill, before leaving Sussex for Oxford where he worked for a firm that made iron lamp posts. In 1917 he had two poems published in a magazine edited by the young T.S. Eliot. Shortly afterwards, Coppard abandoned his job to live alone in a cottage for two years testing his vocation as a writer. The result, in 1921, was his first volume of short stories, *Adam and Eve and Pinch Me*. Coppard spent the rest of his life in the Chilterns and in Essex. When he was over seventy, he wrote the first instalment of an autobiography, *It's Me, O Lord!*, dying while it was in the press. Like some of his stories, *Pomona's Babe*, *Ninepenny Flute* and *The Hundredth Tale*, it vividly paints the Brighton of his childhood. Coppard's reminiscences of his poor beginnings are never disfigured by bitterness, unlike those of Robert Tressell, the house painter who was living in Hastings at about the same time. The difference was that Tressell was a politician, Coppard a poet. Tressell hated the world and wanted to change it; Coppard loved the world and knew it could not be changed.

Lovely vendors also passed the door: the milkman yodelling, the water-cress man with his singsong, the muffin man with tray on head tinkling his bell, the fisherman with a basketful of shrimps or winkles on his arm, or last of all the melancholy midnight howl of the trotter man. Ah, it was a beautiful world, where the shops kept open late and soldiers arrayed like gorgeous gods passed to and fro all day, and men on penny-farthing bicycles toured on roads always coated with dust or thick with lovely mud.

In the past few years the graceful viaduct over the Lewes Road, built in 1869, has been demolished. The Board School that Coppard attended was demolished in 1930 and the present school erected on the same site, in what is now called Fairlight Place. The Barracks in Lewes Road was rebuilt and extended in the 1930s but one of the original blocks survives at the south end of the site. Burdock Farm, Burgess Hill, has vanished under the bricks and mortar of a new estate.

———————————

26. Virginia Woolf *(1882–1941)*

West Firle &
Rodmell

For Virginia Woolf, as for many others, Sussex was a means of survival. Haunted all her life by a fear of madness, she had had severe breakdowns at the age of 13 and 22, attempting suicide by throwing herself from a window. An exhausting bout of work and social engagements in London brought sudden collapses which needed weeks of slow convalescence to repair. In 1910, she decided she must have a country cottage. The house she found was a not very attractive, newly-built, red brick villa in the main street of the village of West Firle, near Lewes. She called it 'Little Talland House' after the house at St Ives in Cornwall where she had spent so many happy childhood holidays. She furnished it and moved in with two servants in the Spring of 1911. She was revising, for the sixth time, her first novel, *The Voyage Out*. She had so far had only book reviews published and sometimes gave way to despair:

> I could not write, and all the devils came out – hairy black ones. To be 29 and unmarried – to be a failure – Childless – insane too, no writer.

Yet she was happy at Firle and walks on the Downs were therapeutic. In April she was well enough to go to Constantinople to admire Byzantine art with Roger Fry and her sister Vanessa and Clive Bell. May and June she spent in her London home, 29 Fitzroy Square. In the autumn walking with Leonard Woolf on the Downs, she was enchanted by her first sight of Asham House, a strangely beautiful gothic house not far from Firle. Shortly afterwards, she and Vanessa took it on a shared lease and in February 1912 Virginia had a house-warming party there; it was an unusually cold winter and all the pipes in the house were frozen.

In the summer of that year Virginia and Leonard were married. Virginia had a severe breakdown and attempted suicide with veronal. Leonard was a devoted nurse, keeping a diary in which he recorded every daily change in her condition. A year later, when she had apparently recovered, they realised their ambition of founding a publishing business: they bought a small hand press and some boxes of type and set up the Hogarth Press at a house in Richmond, Surrey. Shortly afterwards Virginia succumbed to a violent fit of madness and four nurses were brought in to attend her. At Asham, through the summer and autumn of 1915, her mind slowly mended. *The Voyage Out* was published and she was pleased by the critics' reception. Soon the Woolfs were journeying between Asham House and Richmond learning the arts of typesetting and printing. In 1917 their first production appeared – two stories by Virginia and Leonard in a limited edition of 150 copies. 'My only criticism is that there doesn't seem to be quite enough ink' said their friend Lytton Strachey. It was a small beginning; fifty years later the Hogarth Press would publish a complete edition of Freud's works in 24 volumes.

Virginia Woolf   *Asham House, Beddingham*

The Great War made little difference to the lives of the Bloomsberries. In the white-painted rooms of their houses, hung with the works of the Post-Impressionist painters, the endless discussions about the meaning of art and life and politics went on without interruption. Priding themselves on their superior intelligence they were convinced that they were the heralds of a new and more civilised way of life in which patriotism, along with religion and sexual morality, would be left behind as relics of the Victorian Age.

Just after the War the lease of Asham House expired and the Woolfs paid £700 for Monk's House in nearby Rodmell. It was much smaller than Asham and primitive, no bath, no WC, no hot water and brick floors. Its previous owner was an old crazed man who had starved himself to death. Behind the house was a garden and an orchard with overgrown pear and apple trees with views over the flats of the Ouse valley. The physical discomfort of their early years there would daunt most people nowadays.

> We went to Rodmell, and the gale blew at us all day; off arctic fields; so we spent our time attending to the fire.

90

Sometimes Virginia's diary admits that the prospect of another cold weekend at Rodmell was too discouraging so they stayed in London. They were up at 4 a.m. one night chasing mice out of the bed and up again the same night several times to wedge windows banging in the wind. On another night they caught a bat in the bedroom. But always, when the weather was milder, they were drawn irresistibly back: 'We want to get to Rodmell, to see what has happened to the garden. I shall like a soft grey walk. Then the post. Then reading. Then sitting in the chimney corner. I shall walk out on the flats. We take the servants and ensure comfort.'

Apart from some clumsy appearances at village socials, the Woolfs made no attempt to fit in with the local community: they were always 'the gentry' to the villagers. Virginia was secretary of the Rodmell Labour Party whose seven or eight members met in Monk's House, more for village gossip than for political discussion. Virginia preferred it like that; her socialism was only skin-thin and was undertaken to oblige Leonard.

She loathed 'the blasphemy of Peacehaven' and described Newhaven as 'spot and

Virginia Woolf   *Monk's House, Rodmell*

rash and pimple and blister with the incessant motor cars like active lice'. Complaining that Rodmell had become 'a colony of Georgian poets' she wanted to move to Arundel but Leonard dissuaded her. The cottage was more habitable now that £80 had been spent rebuilding the kitchen. In 1925 Virginia set herself 'to make £300 this summer by writing to build a bath and hot water range at Rodmell'. She had a lodge built in the garden where she could write and in 1927 they made the journeys to London easier by buying a Singer car. With profits from the Hogarth Press they bought two cottages in Rodmell to house Percy the gardener and Louie the daily help. They entertained many guests at Monk's House including T.S. Eliot, E.M. Forster, Lytton Strachey, Elizabeth Bowen, and Vita Sackville-West. And in the twenty years at Monk's House Virginia was writing the novels, the essays, the book reviews, the diaries and the letters that now, after her death, fill so many volumes.

At the beginning of 1941 Virginia fell into a mood of deep despair unlike anything Leonard had known before. She had just finished *Between the Acts* and the ending of a novel was always a dangerous time for Virginia. One March day, working in the garden, he went in to lunch and found a letter waiting for him:

> Dearest,
> I feel certain that I am going mad again. I feel we can't go through another of those terrible times. And I shan't recover this time. I begin to hear voices and I can't concentrate. So I am doing what seems the best thing to do.

He found her walking stick on the bank of the Ouse and three weeks later the body was found by some children. She had stuffed a large stone in the pocket of her coat. She was cremated at Brighton and Leonard buried her ashes in the garden. There were two elms there with interlaced boughs that they used to call Leonard and Virginia. About a year after her death one of them was blown down in a gale.

 Monk's House is National Trust property. Driving south from Lewes to Rodmell, make sure to turn left at the Holly Pub and the signpost to Rodmell Church: Monk's House is half-a-mile along on the right. In the summer there are traffic jams in the narrow street with as many as eighty visitors a day to the house, with only 15 people in the house at any one time.

Open: April to the end of October: Wednesday and Saturday only, 2pm–6pm (last admission 5.30pm). Admission charge.

Asham House is opposite Rodmell on the other side of the Ouse. Driving south on the A26 it is about 2 miles from Beddingham. Turn left up a tree-lined drive at road sign 'Beddingham Landfill Site'. Asham House is the subject of Virginia's story The Haunted House. *For Talland House walk down the winding main street of West Firle and look out for a pair of brick houses: the name is on the gate and the date, 1904, above the door.*

27. A.A. Milne *(1882–1956)* Hartfield

I suppose that it will remain the most astonishing day of my life, that February day in 1906, when I entered the *Punch* office, awed but unsuspicious, a casual contributor, with two pounds in the bank, and left it Assistant Editor, with a regular salary.

It was no mean achievement for a young man of twenty-four years. He had left Cambridge with only a third class degree, and his father, headmaster of a private school, had refused to speak to him for a week. Milne had already written some clever light verse and decided to try his luck as a free-lance in Fleet Street. After a few years pestering editors, he was on his feet with £1,000 a year and a growing reputation.

When the Great War came he could view it only as an annoying interruption of a promising career. He had recently married Dorothy de Selincourt, god-daughter of the Editor of *Punch*. She was rich and she laughed at his jokes. As part of the marriage settlement her parents allowed her to take one of their multitudinous servants as a personal maid. Together with a cook, they moved into a comfortable flat on Chelsea Embankment. Undoubtedly one day he would occupy the Editor's chair. But for the time being there was the War. 'I was a pacifist before 1914 but this (I thought with other fools) was a war to end all wars.' He was ready to hate army life but in fact he found it not uncongenial. The influence of a friend ensured that he was commissioned almost as soon as he was in uniform. He trained on the Isle of Wight where he and his wife had the prettiest cottage in Sandown. Here he had sufficient leisure to write his first full-length book, a novel, *Once on a Time*: 'it made the war seem very far away' he wrote. After a brief spell on the Somme he went down with trench fever and was brought back to the Isle of Wight to convalesce. He wrote several plays, some of them produced during wartime. He transferred to Intelligence and finished the war writing propaganda at the War Office.

Back in civvy street he found his desk at *Punch*'s office was occupied. Would he like to submit occasional pieces? At first he agreed but then he found it humiliating and resigned. He would write more plays; *Punch*'s loss would be the English theatre's gain. But in 1920, he and his wife were surprised by the birth of a son, Christopher Robin. On a wet day in Wales, Milne began writing a child's book of verses. *When We Were Very Young* appeared in 1924 and was a great success. The following year he bought Cotchford Farm, a lovely old red-brick farmhouse, on the edge of the Ashdown Forest. From now on, weekends and holidays would be spent in Sussex, driving down from Chelsea in the blue Fiat with Christopher on Nanny's lap. In quick succession there followed *Winnie the Pooh* in 1926, *Now We are Six* in 1927 and *The House at Pooh Corner* in 1928. The next year, Christopher left for boarding school and this extraordinary series of children's books ended.

Extraordinary, for several reasons. Milne himself admitted, 'I am not inordinately fond of or interested in children' and Christopher, in later years, said that his father had no talent for amusing children or for playing with them. When he was not writing, Milne was happiest chasing a ball. The first thing he did at Cotchford was to lay out a clock golf course on the front lawn. A twenty-yard stretch of level grass in the orchard was commandeered as a cricket pitch; later on, a proper pitch was laid in the meadow and practice nets put up. Cricket was taken seriously.

Extraordinary for another reason. In his memoir *The Enchanted Places*, Christopher tells us that because his mother was brought up in a house full of servants she was incapable of doing the smallest thing for herself, even the curtains were drawn by a servant. Unable to cope with the burden of her own child, she handed Christopher over to Nanny; occasionally she would amuse herself for half-an-hour by playing with him. In the Chelsea house the nursery was on the top floor and Christopher ate his meals up there with Nanny instead of with his parents. It is not surprising that his mother and father were almost strangers to him.

> I might not have missed my mother had she disappeared, and would certainly not have missed my father, I would have missed Nanny – most desolately.

Nanny monopolised the boy's affection and there was none left for Milne. Feeling

A.A. Milne

Cotchford Farm, Hartfield

excluded, Milne took refuge in the imagination: he created in his stories another world that compensated him for the disappointments of the real world. He needed the Christopher Robin of his stories because the real Christopher Robin, his own son, was inaccessible to him, That, at least, is what Christopher Robin thinks today, looking back on it all half a century later.

In 1929 Christopher Robin left for boarding school and Nanny left to get married. The Pooh stories had made their author world-famous but Milne felt that enough was enough; he wanted to escape from perpetual servitude to children. In the past he had written some creditable plays, like *Mr Pim Passes By*, and a very good detective story, *The Red House Mystery*. There seemed no reason why he should not write more. He felt about Winnie the Pooh as Conan Doyle about Sherlock Holmes: other, and better work, was being overlooked.

> When I wrote them, little thinking
> All my years of pen-and-inking
> Would be almost lost among
> Those four trifles for the young.

But it was only those 'four trifles' that the public wanted. Throughout the 1930s, Milne wrote plays, novels, stories, verse, but none of it aroused much interest.

Milne was never a man to display his feelings: 'My father's heart remained buttoned up all through his life,' wrote Christopher. In 1940 the Chelsea house in Mallord Street, now number 13 with a plaque on the wall, was sold. Milne went on writing in his small, dark study at Cotchford and the Pooh books went on selling; well over three million to date.

Gills Lap, the Galleon's Lap of the stories, is on the B2026 about three miles south of Hartfield: if you are driving, it is the third Picnic Area on your right. Walk northwards from the car park about 200 yards and you will find the Ordnance Survey obelisk: another 200 yards northwards will bring you to the memorial to Milne and E.H. Shepard, his illustrator, a massive block of rough-hewn stone inscribed to those who 'captured the magic of Ashdown Forest and gave it to the world'. Across the B2026 is Five Hundred Acre Wood, the One Hundred Acre Wood of the stories. On the northern edge of this wood was Owl's House, an ancient beech tree cut down in the last war.

Returning along the B2026, turn left on the B2110 to Gallypot Street, take the second on the left, go to the end and find a track down to the river bottom. Poohsticks Bridge is much the same today as when E.H. Shepard first drew it. Return to where you left the road and continue to follow it. Cotchford, where Milne lived, is on the right-hand side but little of it is visible as its roof is on a level with the road.

28. Andrew Young *(1885–1971)*

Hove, Stonegate &
Yapton

In 1920 Andrew Young left his native Scotland to become minister at the new and imposing red-brick church on the fringe of Brighton. The *Brighton Herald* reported the occasion:

> Mr Young created the most favourable of impressions. He is a young man, clean shaven, with striking features and that air of serene strength that makes a man a leader. He said little, but he said it uncommonly well.

As a comment on Young as a poet as well as a man, that last remark could not be bettered. A reticent man, he had no time for small talk. On the whole he preferred silence to speech. It followed that he was not an easy man to know. It might be thought that he would not be much of a minister. On the contrary: he encouraged his young congregation to read the Greek philosophers and Shakespeare as well as the Bible and would invent detective stories on the spur of the moment, inviting them to solve the mystery.

During the eighteen years that he was at Hove he published ten small volumes of poetry. The first four were small editions of only two hundred copies, now collectors' rarities. Young had no ambition to be famous; a naturally modest man, he made no effort to advertise his work. He was indifferent to literary fashions and read little of the work of his contemporaries. The disillusionment of the 1920s left him untouched and in the 1930s, when other poets were taking up political causes, he kept to his own few acres, never tempted to look over the hedge at the world outside.

His subject matter was anything caught by his sharp eye on a long walk over the downs or across the weald: old chalk quarries, a downland sheep track, a dead rat, a flock of yellow-hammers, lovers' hearts carved on a tree trunk, a field of white flints. Horses still ploughed in Young's Sussex and chiming sheepbells, now an unheard sound, made 'one Sabbath of the years'. Sussex place names are scattered through his Collected Poems: Pevensey, Findon, Cuckmere Haven, Bishopstone, the Adur River, Steyning, Amberley. And so are the names of wild flowers: Young had a lifelong passion for them and it has been said that he saw nearly every wild flower in the British Isles. There are poems on the Night-flowering Campion, Bog Pimpernel, Motherwort, Moth Mullein and many others. In one poem he is hurrying to catch a train at Uckfield but misses it through lingering over the white flowers of spiked rampion. His poems about flowers, small creatures and landscapes are miniature autobiographies, revealing, behind the observant eye, his own faith and his own disquiet.

In 1941 he became vicar of Stonegate at the other end of Sussex, set in the watery world of the Rother valley. It was Andrew Young's home for the next eighteen years. Here, Young was able to slip out of his own time and live the life of a country parson-poet from some more tranquil century. In the winter, rising regularly each day at six o'clock, he devoted himself to writing poetry. His wife protected him from domestic irritations and, if friends stayed too long, it was her practice to tactfully suggest that they might enjoy a visit to Kipling's house at Burwash, a few miles to the south. Occasionally he would go by train to the London Library in St James's Square, taking a small case of books and returning as quickly as he could: he disliked London. In the summer he wrote prose: it was at Stonegate that he wrote *A Prospect of Flowers* and *A Retrospect of Flowers*, books in which he blended scholarship, wisdom and wit. Every summer holiday was spent with his wife in the Highlands of Scotland, climbing mountains in search of wild flowers.

At Stonegate the spring of nature poetry that has flowed so freely for twenty years ran dry. 'I was not sorry,' he wrote, 'for while my interest in nature was intense, it was not as deep as the underlying interest that prompted me to change my style and write *Into Hades*.' This poem and its sequel *A Traveller in Time* took him more than ten years

Andrew Young

Park Lodge, Yapton

to write. In these long and difficult poems, Young attends his own burial in Stonegate churchyard and then explores the life beyond the grave. Although Young regarded these poems as the crown of his life's work they are unlikely ever to displace his nature poems in most readers' hearts.

Young retired at the age of seventy-four: his parishioners thoughtfully gave him a new typewriter to replace the ancient one he had always used. Taking his books and his cherished collection of blue and white china, he and his wife moved into a large old house in Yapton, Park Lodge in Church Lane, a few miles south of Arundel. He wrote three more books of prose: in one of them, *The Poet and the Landscape*, he shares with the reader his delight in his own literary ancestors, the English pastoral poets, Hogg, Crabbe, Clare, Hardy, Wordsworth and many others. It is full of curious learning and antiquarian scholarship and written in his faultless prose. 'You watch words as a cat watches a mouse' said his friend Walter de la Mare.

It was a sad blow when his wife died in 1969. Always a lonely man, he saw friends less often and writing letters, in his tiny, bird's foot-print longhand, was too great an effort. On Sundays he walked to the Norman church at the end of the road, perplexed when the vicar prayed for Bank Holiday travellers on the roads. The garden became overgrown, a haunt for the wild birds he loved.

It was the newspaper boy, pushing the paper through the letterbox, who saw the old man lying in the hall: he had fallen in the night and broken his thigh. Months later he died in a Bognor nursing home. A Canon of Chichester, his funeral was held in the cathedral and his ashes scattered on the neatly barbered grass of the cathedral precincts.

Young's church in Hove, St Cuthbert's, at the corner of Holland and Davigdor Roads, was demolished in 1984. There is a memorial tablet to Young inside the church at Stonegate: it describes him simply as 'Priest, Poet and Naturalist'. The first biography of Young is now being written by his daughter and son-in-law.

29. S.P.B. Mais   *(1885–1975)*

Hove, Southwick &
Shoreham

'Anyone who does not live in Brighton,' said Mais, 'must be mad and ought to be locked up.' Yet, sandwiched between two periods of his long life when he lived on the fringe of Brighton, were nineteen years in Oxford.

He first came to Sussex in 1922: he was thirty-seven and had just married a girl half his age. They took a flat at 22A First Avenue, Hove. Mais was working in Fleet Street as book and theatre critic on some of the leading daily papers. After a first night at a West End theatre, he would rush back to his office, write his piece for the next edition and catch the last train back to Brighton at five minutes past midnight. From Brighton it was a two mile walk or a ten shilling taxi fare to Hove: he usually walked.

Mais had already begun to write books with ease and frequency. He wrote mainly novels, books on the English countryside and books on English literature. Except for an English textbook for schools, which sold 20,000 copies, his books sold sluggishly. His next best was *See England First*, published in 1927. A former public school master, Mais makes the reader feel like an unwilling schoolboy bullied into taking apart in a cross-country race. He devotes no less than a third of the book to the county of Sussex. They are some of the best pages ever written on Sussex. Like Belloc, he walked the county in wet weather and in fine, summer and winter, knowing its trackways, woods and villages with an intimacy achieved only by foot travellers.

Mais wrote several books on counties, including one on Sussex, but it was broadcasting that gave him the public he deserved. He was already a practised lecturer who could hold an audience for an hour without notes, and the BBC asked him to give a series of seventeen talks on the English countryside. Each week he visited somewhere chosen at random on the map, ranging from Tintagel to Inverness, from Anglesey to the Norfolk Broads. The talks were published in 1932 under the title *This Unknown Island*. His warm and friendly voice became familiar in most homes throughout the country.

In 1927 he moved from Hove to Southwick, renting for £100 a year a fine knapped-flint house, built in 1691, known as the Hall, which still stands on Southwick Green. Three years later he lost his job on the *Daily Telegraph* and decided to free-lance as a writer, lecturer and broadcaster. He had a vast appetite for work and it was not unusual for him to be writing a dozen or more books at the same time and to publish eight in one year. He wrote articles for a variety of magazines from the *Nineteenth Century* to *Tit Bits*. He wrote advertising copy for Swan Pens, brochures for hotels, captions for calendars, wrote a history of a steel firm and another of pneumatic tools, and official guides to many resorts including one to Brighton in 1930. He was prodigiously busy on all fronts. There were lecture tours of European countries and a sixteen week broadcasting tour of America. He was commissioned by the Southern

Railway to write booklets of rambles in Kent and Surrey and Sussex and on Sundays he would shepherd trainloads of jaded London office-workers to the top of the South Downs.

Most mornings, before breakfast, he would take the flint track up to the Downs as far as the ancient stone known as the 'Rest and Be Thankful'. If he felt energetic he would go on to the top of Thundersbarrow overlooking Shoreham's tiny harbour.

S.P.B. Mais

The Hall, Southwick Green

After breakfast, in fine weather, he would sit in his front porch with a board across his knees writing and exchanging pleasantries with the passers-by. At noon, he and his family would walk down to Shoreham Beach. He collected old books and old furniture and played cricket on the village green.

Yet it was cricket that forced Mais to leave Southwick. In 1932 the local council tried to stop cricket on the green, alleging that it was dangerous to passers-by. Mais, as President of the Cricket Club, led the opposition. When a match was banned by the council, the teams turned up and after their names had been solemnly recorded in the village policemen's notebook, they played their match. Threats of legal action did not deter Mais: if necessary, he said, he would appeal to the House of Lords. Mais revelled in the publicity and saw himself as a village Hampden. But he overplayed his hand when he refused to pay his rates to the dictatorial council: he was prosecuted and evicted. Meanwhile, a new council was elected that reversed the decision of its predecessor. Mais had won the battle for cricket on Southwick Green but had lost his lovely house.

For £150 a year, Mais rented a new, red-brick house in Shoreham, at the junction of Buckingham Road and the Upper Shoreham Road, which he called Toad Hall. The growing expense of a family, with a nurse, a daily help and the education of his two girls, Imogen and Lalage, kept Mais hard at work. Much of his time was spent away from home, collecting material for travel books, broadcasting and lecturing.

When the war came, Shoreham harbour and airport were daily targets for German bombers so Mais took his family back to his childhood home, the Rectory at Tansley, a mining village in Derbyshire. After a year, his father, an irascible old clergyman in his eighties, threw them out and they moved to Oxford. They kept Toad Hall for many years, always hoping to return, but eventually gave it up: the house still retains its old name.

It was twenty years before Mais came back to Sussex, to a flat at 38A Brunswick Square in Hove. To celebrate his return he was invited to bring a combined BBC and Oxford and Cambridge cricket team to play against Southwick on the village green. When he died, at the age of ninety, he was living in a flat at Lindfield, Haywards Heath, but he always thought of Southwick as his home. At the end of his autobiography, he writes:

> If I am privileged as a ghost to revisit the glimpses of the moon perhaps you'd like my address. It will be:
>
>   The Village Green,
>   Southwick,
>   Sussex.
> And I'll tell you where exactly on the green I shall be in case you want to exchange greetings. I shall be hovering over the oak seat which bears the inscription:
>   'Given by Lalage and Imogen Mais'

The seat has now gone but the spirit of SPB is still there. His best memorial is the fact that cricket is still played on Southwick Green.

'Famous Novelist Builds a Church' was the headline in a national paper in 1935. Except for one brief phase in her twenties, when she toyed with Nietzsche and Madame Blavatsky, Sheila Kaye-Smith was always deeply attracted by Catholicism. Her mother was Presbyterian and her father, a doctor with a local practice, was a conventional Anglican. When they found their daughter slipping into Christ Church, St Leonard's, on her way home from school, they strongly disapproved. Christ Church was a stronghold of Anglo-Catholicism and renowned for its liturgical splendours. Her furtive visits meant a lot to Sheila; she loved the 'warm, incense-smelling shadows, full of winking red lights'.

Religion was one thread in her life; love of place was another. Born in Hastings, she was to spend most of her life in the lovely wooded valleys of the Rother, Brede and Tillingham Rivers. In her autobiography, *Three Ways Home*, she remembered the holidays of childhood at Platnix Farm between Westfield and Sedlescombe:

> It was the first twelve years of my life that made me a Sussex novelist. I still write, I know, from the impressions of those early days – pictures that I always see in a clear sunshine, vivid, slight, and sharp as swords in my memory. In a sense every farm I write of is Platnix Farm, and every human being is one or another of the people that I met there. My very earliest imagination was captured by the countryside that holds it still.

She is Sussex's only regional novelist and in 1983 Virago reissued two of her novels, *Joanna Godden* and *Susan Spray*. A reading of almost any of her books can enrich a visit to her part of East Sussex.

She wrote with great facility from an early age. During her last two years at school she produced thirteen novelettes written in pencil in dozens of penny exercise books. Her model was Edna Lyall, a now forgotten writer of historical romances who was also a devout Anglican. At the age of twenty-one Sheila Kaye-Smith achieved local notoriety with her first published novel, *The Tramping Methodist*, considered unladylike because of its murder trial and lurid prison scenes. It was followed six months later by a second. She soon schooled herself to write a full-length novel in six to nine months. At first they sold in hundreds but gradually her sales mounted and with *Green Apple Harvest* in 1920, sales reached four figures, and in the next year came *Joanna Godden*, a story of the Romney Marshes that was filmed with Googie Withers as the heroine. In 1923 *The End of the House of Alard* became a best-seller both here and in America. It made her rich over-night: 'I had more money than I had ever had in my life.'

The background to this novel was her return to the 'warm, incense-smelling shadows' of Christ Church, St Leonard's. There, in 1918, she made her first confession and became an Anglo-Catholic, eager to do her part to restore Catholic

Sheila Kaye-Smith   Little Doucegrove, Northiam

practices to the Church of England. Religious conversion can have a damaging effect on a novelist: with Sheila Kaye-Smith it intensified her vision of the natural world. 'I saw a beauty in the Sussex fields that I seemed hitherto only to have guessed at. The country of Westfield and Brede and Udimore, Platnix and the River Tillingham had been baptized into the same reality as I.' The novel about the Alards was the first in which she made explicit her Anglo-Catholicism. Its hero is a young man who is heir to the family estate but renounces it to enter a monastery. It made her popular with the leaders of the Anglo-Catholic movement in England which had recently suffered the loss of G.K. Chesterton to Rome and wanted another 'big name' speaker. She was never much of a speaker but she did her best. She wrote a good book entitled *Anglo-Catholicism*.

In 1924 she married Penrose Fry, the curate at Christ Church. The Rector preferred celibate curates so her husband took another curacy in a parish in Kensington. Although she was living for the first time outside Sussex, the flow of novels was uninterrupted. But both she and her husband were uneasy with their position in the Church of England. They had begun to realise that it was but a half-way house on the road to Rome. She felt that as an Anglo-Catholic she was a 'synthetic Catholic'. In 1928 they visited Palermo in Sicily and went to a colourful and tumultuous Mass in the cathedral. In 1925 there was the canonization of St Thérèse of Lisieux, a saint who had made a deep impression on her: there is an essay on St Thérèse in her book *Quartet in Heaven*. Her husband's doubts led him to resign his curacy, leaving them free to move back to Sussex. In 1929 they bought the isolated and ruined oasthouse, Little Doucegrove, between Northiam and Brede. With it went some fifty acres of grass, woodland and unkempt orchards and it needed a great deal of work to make it habitable. Shortly afterwards there was another homecoming: after receiving instruction from Father Martindale, who lived nearby at Rye, she and her husband were received into the Roman Catholic Church.

Doucegrove was nine miles from the nearest Catholic Church and there were Catholics scattered about her neighbourhood who found it too far to travel. She converted a loft above the stables into an oratory – she called it the Upper Room – and persuaded a priest to come once a quarter to say Mass. The Southwark Travelling Mission helped by sending their van round to collect the lapsed Catholics from the lonely homesteads. The quarterly Mass became monthly and then weekly. Sheila Kaye-Smith took on the 'parish work' of visiting the sick, teaching the children their catechism and other duties. As the years passed, the congregation outgrew the tiny oratory and when death-watch beetles made the floor of the Upper Room unsafe, she provided the land and the money to build a small church nearby. In December 1935, five years exactly after Mass had first been said in the Upper Room, the Church of St Thérèse of Lisieux was opened. Its first priest, Father Currie, was still priest in 1983, though he was eighty-five and a heart attack had confined him to a nursing home. Sheila Kaye-Smith died when she fell down the spiral staircase in the converted oast kiln that was her study. She was buried in the graveyard of her own church.

Driving north up the A28, watch out after passing through Broad Oak for the Tanhouse Farm oast house on the corner of the turning to Doucegrove. After leaving the A28 take the first left; the church is on the left and the house is at the end of the lane. Just before reaching the house you will see a row of cottages with a stable, now a garage, at the near end: above this was the Upper Room.

Returning to the A28, turn south and Conster Manor, the family home of the Alards in The End of the House of Alard, *is about a mile along the road on the left. The Alard's ancestors lie in Winchelsea Churchyard. R. Thurston Hopkins has done a fascinating bit of detective work in his book* Sheila Kaye-Smith and the Weald Country *(1925). Finally, no one should venture into this part of Sussex without taking with them Kaye-Smith's own delightful guide book,* Weald of Kent and Sussex, *reprinted in 1966: an invaluable companion.*

31. Mervyn Peake *(1911–1968)*   Burpham

It was the last war that brought Mervyn Peake, painter and poet, and his wife Maeve, to Sussex. His parents had already moved there and built a house for their retirement in the secluded village of Burpham. Mervyn and Maeve had spent their honeymoon at the house in 1937 and when the war began, as Maeve was expecting a baby, they decided to leave their Maida Vale studio and find somewhere safe from Hitler's bombs. They rented a small thatched cottage in Warningcamp, a mile or so from Reed Thatch, the parents' house. The cottage was damp, candle-lit and haunted: romantic in summer but uncomfortable in the winter. They arrived in January and later that month, in Littlehampton Hospital, Maeve had a son, Sebastian. Dr Peake planted a willow tree in the front garden of Reed Thatch to celebrate the birth.

Mervyn had tried to get work as a war artist but without success: a letter from Augustus John on his behalf had been ignored. His call-up papers came and when the baby was two-weeks old he had to leave for training as a gunner at Dartmouth. He and Maeve walked to Arundel Station along the tow-path, facing, as so many young couples did in wartime, their first separation. He did his best to fit himself, a square peg, into an impossibly round hole. He had an enviable ability to detach himself from alien surroundings and get on with his work of drawing or writing. The difficulty of setting up an easel in a barrack-room forced him to abandon painting and concentrate on book-illustration. In barracks, crowded cafés, in the company of friends, his notebook would be on his knee, filled with his neat handwriting, with sketches of the faces around him, or with strange visionary creatures.

Most of Peake's first novel, *Titus Groan*, was written like that – in small ruled exercise books. When they were full they were sent to Maeve to be read and talked over on his next leave and finally to be stored by her bedside. But the book began in the damp cottage by the bank of the Arun, Gormenghast Castle sprouting in Peake's imagination from the sight of the massive grey walls and turrets of Arundel Castle high up on the opposite bank of the river.

Gunner Peake 5917577 was stationed first at Dartmouth, then on ack-ack guns on the Isle of Sheppey and then, when it was discovered that he could drive, in Blackpool. Here he was joined by Maeve and Sebastian in a billet, a couple of rooms where Mervyn wrote *Titus Groan* in the evening while downstairs RAF men played Glenn Miller's 'In The Mood' endlessly on a piano. In the summer of 1941, he was transferred to a bomb disposal unit in London and stationed at the Duke of York's Barracks in Chelsea. Later in that year, *Shapes and Sounds*, his first collection of poetry was published, in a jacket designed by himself. In December there was an exhibition of his drawings in London, including the originals of his illustrations to Lewis Carroll's *The Hunting of the Snark*, which had appeared earlier in the year.

Meanwhile Maeve had exchanged the damp cottage by the river for three rooms on the top floor of the School House in Upper Warningcamp; the tenant of the house was formerly cook to Maeve's mother. About a year later there was another move to a cottage next door to Reed Thatch, known as 94, Wepham. On higher ground, it was drier and warmer than their first cottage. The rent was three shillings a week.

In April 1942 Maeve had a second son, Fabian. Mervyn applied for compassionate leave to visit her but was refused. Putting his talent as a draughtsman to good use, he forged a pass and arrived just after the birth. He returned to face a charge of AWOL – absent without leave. The Army doctors decided that he was suffering a nervous breakdown and sent him to a Neurosis Centre at Southport. Peake's mental state at this time is difficult to assess but it did not interfere with the writing of *Titus Groan*; chapters 56 and 57 were both written at the Centre and Peake even persuaded the Matron to type out some of the manuscript. In September 1942, after six months 'treatment', he was sent home to Burpham on indefinite sick leave. In April of the next year he was invalided out of the Army.

Mervyn Peake   *94 Wepham, Burpham*

Peake now settled down in the cottage to finish *Titus Groan*. When it was done he sent it to his friend Graham Greene who was then working for the publishers Eyre and Spottiswoode. Greene was not the sort of man to let friendship soften his criticism: he wrote a 'mercilessly frank' letter to Peake explaining what needed to be done to make the book publishable. Peake worked hard at revising the text but it was not until February 1946 that the book was published – six years after its birth in the damp cottage by Arun River. There was other work too, commissions for book illustrations and paintings for the Ministry of Information. His seven illustrations for Coleridge's *Rime of the Ancient Mariner*, done in his Burpham period, are probably the finest he ever did.

In the summer of 1944 their tenancy of the cottage expired and they were unable to renew it. Leaving Burpham, they took a studio in Chelsea. They never returned to Sussex to live but were frequent visitors to Reed Thatch to stay with old Dr Peake and, after his death, with Lonnie, Mervyn's brother, who inherited the house. Between 1954 and 1956 Peake taught illustration at the Brighton College of Art and often stayed overnight at Burpham.

It was at this time that Peake was found to be suffering from Parkinson's Disease and the last ten years of his life were darkened by the gradual enfeeblement of his mind and body. Towards the end, in an Oxfordshire nursing home, he no longer wanted to draw or write and was often unable to recognise Maeve. He was buried in Burpham churchyard where his father and mother already lay: on his gravestone is inscribed a line from one of his poems:

To live at all is miracle enough.

Dr. Peake's house Reed Thatch is about two miles along the road to Burpham from the A27; it is on the left-hand side and the name is clearly marked. The thatch caught fire on April Fool's Day 1951 and was replaced with tiles. Mervyn's cottage is next door with 94 on the gate post. A few years ago the thatch suffered the same fate and was replaced with old weathered tiles.

———————————

32. James Hurdis *(1763–1801)*

Educated Chichester and Oxford. In 1784 became curate at Burwash. the long poem *The Village Curate* being his most popular work. He was born in the medieval house 'Little Tallands' at Norton, just north of Bishopstone and went back to live there when he became vicar of Bishopstone.

James Hurdis   *Bishopstone Church*

33. Harrison Ainsworth *(1805–1882)*

Brighton

When 29 his romance *Rookwood* made him the darling of London's literary salons, and many historical travel books ensued. A wide circle of literary and artistic friends: Bulwer-Lytton, Thackeray, Cruickshank, Landseer and an impecunious journalist named Charles Dickens. He lived at 5 Arundel Terrace, on Brighton's sea-front for many years.

34. Mark Lemon *(1809–1870)*   Crawley

The first editor of *Punch* (founded 1841) who was keen to succeed as a serious novelist, but failed.

35. Coventry Patmore *(1823–1896)*   Herons Ghyll & Hastings

His collection of poems *The Angel in the House* (1854), which celebrated the joys of married love, became a great Victorian favourite, selling more than a quarter of a million copies. He lived at what is now Temple Grove School, Herons Ghyll and then at Mansion House, High St, Hastings.

36. Mark Rutherford *(1830–1913)*   Hastings

'Mark Rutherford' was a pseudonym for W.H. White, a high ranking Admiralty official. A novelist and biographer of Bunyan, he married for the second time at the age of eighty-one. He lived for eight years at 7 High Wickham on Hastings' East Cliff, where there is now a plaque on the wall.

37. Richard Jefferies *(1848–1887)*   Hove & Goring

A constant visitor to Sussex, Jefferies settled there for his last five years before dying from consumption. A naturalist and visionary mystic. He lived at 87 Lorna Rd, Hove. He died in Jefferies House, Jefferies Lane, Goring-by-Sea. It is a private house but can be viewed by arrangement with Mr. W. Griffiths; telephone Worthing 43599.

Richard Jefferies
Jefferies' House, Goring-by-sea

38. W.E. Henley *(1849–1903)*   Worthing

An influential editor who first published Kipling in his weekly magazine. Similarly supported H.G. Wells, Conrad, Hardy and Yeats. He once wrote a patriotic poem commemorating the beginning of the Boer War for the *Daily Mail*. He lived for three years in what is now St George's Lodge Hotel, Chesswood Rd, Worthing.

39. John Oxenham *(1852–1941)*   Worthing

Helped Jerome K. Jerome to launch the magazine *The Idler* but then left Fleet Street to write over 40 romantic novels. In 1913 his publisher turned down a small collection of religious verse. Oxenham published it himself and by 1940 *Bees in Amber* had sold over a quarter of a million copies. He lived at 20 Farncombe Rd, Worthing, which is now demolished.

40. J. Horace Round *(1854–1928)*   Hove

The founder of the science of historical genealogy. Always aroused hostility and controversy in his provocative historical writing. Was born and died in the magnificent Brunswick Terrace, number 15, where his father and grandfather had lived before him.

J. Horace Round   _Brunswick Terrace, Hove_

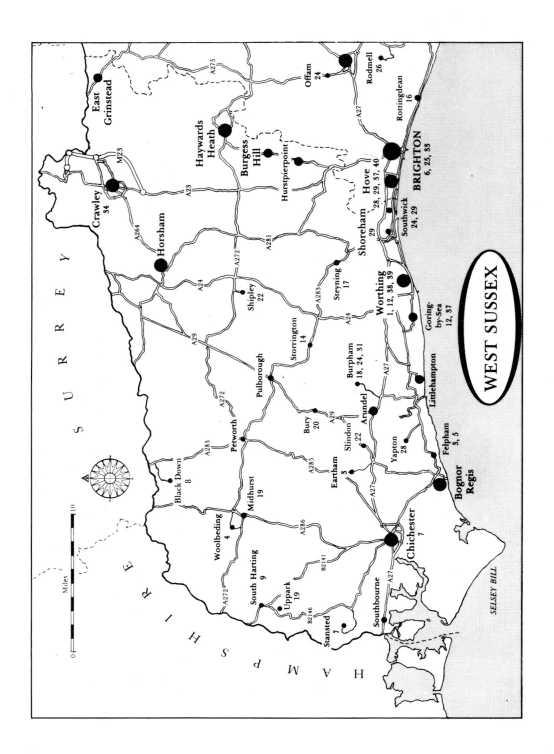

WEST SUSSEX

SURREY

HAMPSHIRE

East
Grinstead

Crawley
34

Horsham

Haywards
Heath

Burgess
Hill

Hurstpierpoint

Offam
24

Rodmell
26

Rottingdean
16

BRIGHTON
6, 25, 33

Hove
28, 29, 37, 40

Shoreham
29

Southwick
24, 29

Worthing
1, 12, 38, 39

Goring-
by-Sea
12, 37

Steyning
17

Shipley
22

Storrington
14

Pulborough

Bury
20

Slindon
22

Burpham
18, 24, 31

Arundel

Yapton
28

Littlehampton

Felpham
3, 5

Bognor
Regis

Black Down
8

Petworth

Midhurst
19

Eartham
3

Woolbeding
4

South Harting
9

Uppark
19

Stansted
7

Southbourne

Chichester
7

SELSEY BILL

M23

A275

A27

A23

A264

A281

A272

A24

A283

A24

A27

A29

A29

A285

A283

A272

A286

A272

B2141

B2146

A27

Miles

0 10

112

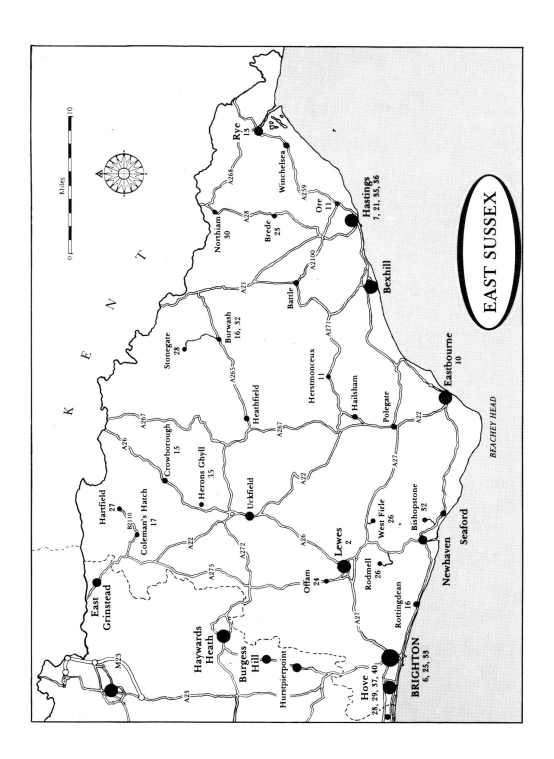

EAST SUSSEX

Rye 13
Winchelsea
Northiam 30
Brede 23
Ore 11
Hastings 7, 21, 35, 36
Battle
Bexhill
Burwash 16, 32
Stonegate 28
Herstmonceux 11
Heathfield
Hailsham
Eastbourne 10
Polegate
BEACHEY HEAD
Crowborough 15
Herons Ghyll 35
Uckfield
Harfield 27
Coleman's Hatch 17
West Firle 26
Bishopstone 32
Lewes 2
Rodmell 26
Seaford
East Grinstead
Offam 24
Rottingdean 16
Newhaven
Haywards Heath
Burgess Hill
Hurstpierpoint
Hove 28, 29, 37, 40
BRIGHTON 6, 25, 33

KENT

Miles
0   10

113

Further Reading

Ainsworth, H.	*W.H. Ainsworth* by S.M. Ellis (1911)
Belloc. H.	*Life of Hilaire Belloc* by Robert Spaeight (1957)
	Hilaire Belloc: a Memoir by J.B. Morton (1955)
	Hilaire Belloc by A.N. Wilson (1984)
Blake, W.	*Blake's Hayley* by Morchard Bishop (1951)
Coppard, A.E.	*It's Me, O Lord!* by A.E. Coppard (1957)
Crane, S.	*Stephen Crane* by John Berryman (1950)
Doyle, A.C.	*The Life of Sir Arthur Conan Doyle* by John Dickson Carr (1969 reprint)
Galsworthy, J.	*Galsworthy: a Biography* by Catherine Dupre (1976)
	Galsworthy by Sheila Kaye-Smith (1916)
Hare, A.	*The Years with Mother* by Augustus Hare, edited by Malcolm Barnes (1952)
	In My Solitary Life by Augustus Hare, edited by Malcolm Barnes (1952)
Hayley, W.	*Memoirs of the Life and Writings of William Hayley Esq. the Friend and Biographer of Cowper* by W. Hayley (new edition 1972)
Henley, W.E.	*W.E. Henley* by John Connell (1949)
Hudson, W.H.	*W.H. Hudson* by Ruth Tomalin (1982)
	Nature in Downland by W.H. Hudson (1906)
Hurdis, J.	*James Hurdis: His Life and Writings* by A.P. Whitaker (1960)
Huxley, T.H.	*Life & Letters of T.H. Huxley* by Leonard Huxley (1900)
James, H.	*Henry James at Home* by Montgomery Hyde (1969)
Jefferies, R.	*Richard Jefferies, His Life & Work* by Edward Thomas (1909; new edition 1978)
Kaye-Smith, S.	*Three Ways Home* by Sheila Kaye-Smith (1937)
Keats, J.	*John Keats: The Living Year* by Robert Gittings (1954)
Kipling, R.	*Rudyard Kipling* by Charles Carrington (1978)
	Kipling's Sussex Revisited by R. Thurston Hopkins (1929)
Lemon, M.	*Mark Lemon* by Arthur A. Adrian (1966)
Mais, S.P.B.	*All The Days of My Life* by S.P.B. Mais (1937)
	Buffets and Rewards by S.P.B. Mais (1952)
Milne, A.A.	*It's Too Late Now* by A.A. Milne (1939)
	Enchanted Places by Christopher Milne (1974)
Oxenham, J.	*J.O.* by Erica Oxenham (1942)
Paine, T.	*Rebel* by Samuel Edwards (1974)
Patmore, C.	*The Life & Times of Coventry Patmore* by Derek Patmore (1949)
Peake, M.	*Mervyn Peake* by John Watney (1976)
	A World Away by Maeve Gilmore (1970)
Pound, E.	*Life of Ezra Pound* by Noel Stock (1970)

Powys, J.C.	*Autobiography* by John Cowper Powys (1934)
	The Brothers Powys by Richard Perceval Graves (1983)
Round, J.H.	*Family Origins and Other Studies* by J. Horace Round, with a Memoir by William Page (1930)
Rutherford, M.	*Mark Rutherford* by Catherine Maclean (1955)
	Autobiography & Deliverance of Mark Rutherford (1969)
Smith, H.	*James & Horace Smith* by A.H. Beavan (1899)
Tennyson, A.	*Tennyson: Poet & Prophet* by Philip Henderson (1978)
Thompson, F.	*Francis Thompson & Wilfred Meynell: a Memoir* by Viola Meynell (1952)
Tressell, R.	*One of the Damned* by F.C. Ball (1973)
Trollope, A.	*Autobiography* by A. Trollope (reprinted 1953)
	Trollope by C.P. Snow (1975)
Wells, H.G.	*Experiment in Autobiography* (1934)
Woolf, V.	*The Journey not the Arrival Matters* by Leonard Woolf (1969)
	Virginia Woolf by Quentin Bell (1972)
Yeats, W.B.	*W.B. Yeats* by Joseph Hone (1942)
	Yeats, Pound and Eliot: Sailing Into the Unknown by Rosenthal (1978)
Young, A.	*Andrew Young: Prospect of a Poet* edited by L. Clark (1957)

Index

Italicised numbers indicate illustrations

Two contemporary 'Sussex writers' published by Redcliffe: Keith Clements and Derek Stanford

Henry Lamb
The Artist and his Friends
by Dr. Keith Clements

The full story of Lamb's life and an assessment of his work is long overdue.

The man and the artist have been rediscovered from a wealth of unpublished material and extensive interviews with family, friends and collectors. It is a remarkably frank and intimate portrait of a very private person and is a critical biography which fills a significant and considerable gap in the life and letters of the period.

The story sheds new light on Bloomsbury and Fitzrovia, and Lamb's turbulent relationships with Lytton Strachey, Ottoline Morrell, Virginia Woolf and Stanley Spencer are spotlighted for the first time.

Dr Keith Clements is Senior Lecturer in Art History at Brighton Polytechnic, specialising in twentieth century British Art.

Casebound   350pp   8 colour / 40 b/w plates   £16.50

The Vision and Death of Aubrey Beardsley
by Derek Stanford

In this unique dramatic monologue, Derek Stanford brings the world's most notorious black and white artist back to life.

Closely based on biographical fact, even at times employing the artist's own words, the author traces his obsessions with art, sex and later, Catholicism. We witness his brushes with Oscar Wilde, John Lane and the turbulent passage of the Yellow Book.

This psychological reconstruction, nourished by the author's special knowledge of the period, produces a portrait, a poem, which reaches beyond traditional limits.

Derek Stanford, author of many books on the 1890s period, lives and works in Brighton, where Beardsley himself was born and brought up.

Publication: October 1985

120